We hope you enjoy this book.
Please return or renew it by the due date.
You can renew it at **www.norfolk.gov.uk/libraries**
or by using our free library app. Otherwise you can
phone **0344 800 8020** - please have your library
card and pin ready.
You can sign up for email reminders too.

LST/CM

Disney · PIXAR
CHARACTER ENCYCLOPEDIA
NEW EDITION

CONTENTS

This character encyclopedia features more than 290 of Disney•Pixar's best-loved characters, from fearless Finn McMissile to Remy the rodent, from brave Buzz Lightyear to big, bad Bruce the Shark and many more. The book is organised in chronological order, from *Toy Story* to *Coco*, with any sequels such as *Toy Story 4* included with the original movie. Look below to find your favourite!

WOODY

HOWDY! SHERIFF WOODY is a rootin', tootin' cowboy doll who is smart, funny and kind. For years, Woody is the leader of the toys in Andy's bedroom, but when he is donated to Bonnie he becomes part of a larger, blended gang. Woody doesn't quite have the same role he used to, but he is determined to be there for Bonnie, just as he was for Andy.

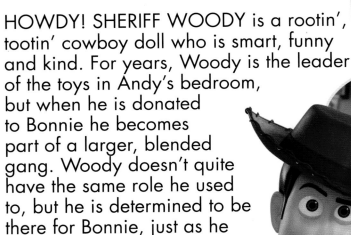

Time for a change
With Andy all grown up, the toys panic about what might happen to them. Woody is sure that Andy will look after them, but when the toys are accidentally put out with the rubbish, no one believes him.

Sheriff's badge

"What matters is we're here for Andy when he needs us."

Rodeo-themed belt buckle

Best buddies
Woody is Andy's favourite toy until Buzz Lightyear shows up. At first, Woody is deeply suspicious of the space ranger, but the two toys eventually become the best of friends and Andy loves them both.

Empty holster

Top toy
Woody was once a famous toy, and the star of the black and white TV show *Woody's Roundup*. Nowadays, he is a valuable collector's item, but Woody knows that the most important thing for any toy is to be loved by a kid.

New gang
Woody always saves the day! He has the perfect solution to the gang's problem, and works out a way to get Andy to donate them to a loving girl named Bonnie. Now the gang has a new home and toys to hang out with. Sheriff Woody's next task? To find Bonnie's newest toy Forky.

BUZZ LIGHTYEAR

THIS SPACE RANGER comes in peace. Buzz is quite simply the coolest toy in the universe! With his best pal Woody by his side, brave Buzz can take on anything, from nasty neighbours to creepy collectors and even a surprise change of kid. This high-tech toy is also a whizz with gadgets and a natural problem solver.

Facing the truth
When Buzz first arrives, he thinks he's a real space ranger. Woody tries to tell him that he's a toy, but Buzz doesn't believe him – until he sees a Buzz Lightyear commercial. The truth hits Buzz hard.

Space ranger logo

"This isn't flying, it's falling with style!"

El Buzzo
When Buzz is accidentally reset from demo mode to Spanish mode, his personality changes dramatically. He becomes romantic, poetic and loves to dance! Jessie kind of likes the new Buzz!

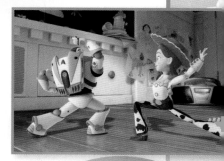

Bendable knee joints

Above and beyond
Buzz would go to infinity and beyond for his pals – he's just that kind of toy. However, two toys hold an extra-special place in the space ranger's heart – his pal Woody and the feisty, red-haired cowgirl Jessie.

Did You Know?
When Woody goes missing while looking for Forky, Bonnie's lost toy, Buzz launches a bold rescue attempt. To the carnival – and possibly beyond!

HAMM

TOY 4
TOY 3
TOY 2
TOY

ANDY'S PIGGY BANK Hamm is much more than just a cute way of storing loose change. The clever swine is always the first to know what's happening in the outside world. While the other toys rush headlong into adventures, sensible Hamm can usually be seen with his snout in an instruction manual.

Dr Porkchop

In Andy's games, Hamm plays the evil Dr Porkchop, but his wicked plans are always foiled by Andy's heroes – Woody and Buzz.

Child's play

Hamm is used to role playing, but the kids at Sunnyside Daycare are too much for the put–upon pig. Being dunked in glue and covered with glitter and macaroni is just not a good look for him!

"You heard of Kung Fu? Well, get ready for pork chop!"

Pig pals

Hamm is good friends with Mr Potato Head. The cynical pair share a love of wisecracks, playing poker and expecting the worst in every situation. At Bonnie's house, Hamm finds a new pal in Buttercup. Finally, he has a buddy as brainy as himself!

Slot for loose change

Pink, plastic body

Trusty trotters

SLINKY

SLINKY DOG IS a toy's best friend, and the coiled canine will go to any lengths to help his pals, especially Sheriff Woody. When he's not on dog duty, Slinky likes to relax by playing draughts with Woody. However, sometimes his loyalties can be as flexible as his body.

Divided loyalties
When Buzz arrives, Slinky is impressed by his gadgets. He forgets all about Sheriff Woody for a while.

Streeeeetch
Slinky's body comes in very handy. He is springier than a ladder and stretchier than a rope. He even makes a great fence!

"I knew you were right all along, Woody."

Springy tail

Faithful friend
Slinky is a simple, straightforward kind of hound, so when he sees Woody "injure" Buzz, he turns against his cowboy chum. However, he soon realises the truth and doesn't hesitate to spring into action and save Woody.

Extendable body

MR POTATO HEAD

THIS STRAIGHT-TALKING spud is one of the funniest toys in Andy's room. He has a smart mouth (when it's not falling off) and a hard-boiled personality. However, underneath Mr Potato Head's grumpy exterior is a sensitive guy who just needs the love of a good potato woman.

Versatile veggie
Thanks to his detachable body parts, Mr Potato Head can convey a range of emotions. He also loves to amuse his fellow toys with his clever impressions, such as Potato Picasso.

Ages 3 and up!
Mr P. H. has always been sensitive about who plays with him. After a toddler play session at Sunnyside Daycare, he feels completely mashed.

"That's Mister Potato Head to you!"

Quizzical eyebrows

Stylish hat

Did You Know?
Mr Potato Head likes to relax by playing poker with his pal, Hamm. Of course, he is a very bad loser!

Tempestuous tater
In Andy's games, Mr Potato Head plays the tough bad guy, One-Eyed Bart, but it's not all an act. He has a quick temper and can often jump to the wrong conclusion about his fellow toys.

MRS POTATO HEAD

THIS ROMANTIC ROOT vegetable is devoted to her husband. In her (detachable) eyes, he is the perfect potato and just needs to be looked after. However, Mrs Potato Head is no pushover. If Mr P. H. steps out of line, he can expect a real roasting from the missus.

One potato, two potato
For years, Mr Potato Head dreamed of a Mrs Potato Head to share his life with. The devoted pair really are made for each other.

Detachable daisy

"They're so adorable. Let's adopt them!"

Keep an eye out
Having detachable body parts has its advantages. When Mrs Potato Head leaves one of her eyes in Andy's room, she is able to tell the other toys that Andy didn't really mean to dump them.

Detachable earrings

Earth Mum
Mrs Potato Head is not only fiercely loyal to her husband, she would also do anything to protect their adopted children. The soft-hearted spud is unofficial mum to three quirky, squishy Aliens, and, most recently, Bonnie Anderson's cheeky Peas-in-a-Pod.

Did You Know?
Mrs Potato Head belongs to Andy's sister, Molly, but she lives in Andy's room with her husband.

REX

HE MIGHT LOOK fierce, but Rex is a timid toy who is anxious about everything. He worries that he isn't scary enough, that his roar is too quiet and that his arms are too short, but Rex's biggest fear is that Andy will find a replacement dinosaur. However, the prehistoric panicker is stronger and braver than he realises.

Fast fingers

Rex is an obsessive video gamer. His favorite is the Buzz Lightyear game, although he can't press the "fire" and "jump" buttons at the same time due to his small arms.

A sad tail

Rex's long tail is always knocking things over. He just can't control it! Mr Potato Head gave him the nickname "Godspilla".

"At last! I'm gonna get played with!"

Dino hero

Rex wishes he was more fierce and fearsome, but the rest of the gang wouldn't have him any other way. After all, he once saved them from the evil Emperor Zurg and helped them to escape from a rubbish bag bound for the bin.

Tiny arms

Scaly, plastic skin

Big, clumsy feet

BO PEEP

PORCELAIN SHEPHERDESS Bo Peep is a loyal friend to Sheriff Woody and stands by him when the other toys think he has hurt Buzz. When the lamp she is part of is given away, resourceful Bo starts a new life as a lost toy rescuer. She travels around meeting kids at carnivals, schools and summer camps. She has more friends than ever before.

Crook

Repair to arm

Skirt worn as cape

Great acting

Bo plays the damsel in distress in Andy's Wild West games, but in reality she needs no help from anyone to survive. In fact, Bo turns out to be a red-hot rescuer herself.

Did You Know?

Bo Peep's porcelain sheep are far from sheepish. The feisty flock help chase off Bo's enemies (when they aren't getting lost!).

"You're cute when you care."

Dressed for action

A dainty dress is fine for a porcelain figure on Molly's lamp, but a travelling toy rescuer needs something more practical. Flouncy skirts can be hard to run in! Bo's comfy blue jumpsuit gives her much more freedom.

11

SARGE AND THE SOLDIERS

THE GREEN ARMY Men may be the smallest toys in the toy box, but these highly trained plastic soldiers are ready to face any challenge with teamwork, determination and good old-fashioned courage. Sarge is the leader of the Bucket o' Soldiers, and they are all very loyal to him.

Roger that!
Communication is important for any good army. The Green Army Men commandeer Molly's baby monitor to use as a radio on their top secret missions.

Sarge in charge
The obedient soldiers obey Sarge's orders without hesitation. At his command, the army men will leap from their bucket, parachute down stairs, move heavy equipment or form an all-out attack.

Binoculars

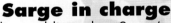

Get him!
The loyal troops don't question the order to swarm Woody when Sarge thinks he has deliberately pushed Buzz out of the window.

"It's been an honour serving with you."

Did You Know?
It's not easy for Sarge and the Green Army Men to get around because their feet are stuck to plastic bases. But they don't let that stop them!

Plastic base

RC

THIS REMOTE-CONTROLLED car is the fastest toy in Andy's room. In fact, RC has two speeds – fast and turbo! Any chance he gets, RC can be seen speeding, swerving and skidding around Andy's room – the word "slow" just isn't in his vocabulary. RC has even been known to go off road!

Rev it up!

RC can't talk, but he conveys his emotions by revving his engine. It means he is either excited or scared. That's how he tells the other toys that Woody has "pushed" Buzz out of the window.

Teamwork

RC's speed and Slinky's stretching abilities nearly succeed in reuniting the toys, but RC's batteries give out at the crucial moment.

Remote-control antenna

Turbo hero

RC makes up for being wrong about Woody. He tries to give him and Buzz a ride so they can catch up with the moving truck when the other toys have to leave without them.

Remote ride

RC sometimes gives the other toys a ride. Buzz and Woody have both been in the driver's seat, but they are powerless to stop RC's batteries from draining. If they run out, the ride is over!

Eye-shaped headlights

Rubber tyres

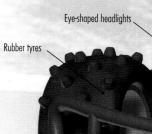

LENNY

A PAIR OF WIND-UP child's binoculars, Lenny is more than just a toy. Thanks to his magnifying lenses, he can see further than any of the other toys in Andy's room, which makes him the perfect lookout. Lenny is also small and lightweight enough for the other toys to use, and he is always willing to lend his pals a helping eye.

Seeing the truth
Lenny calls it exactly as he sees it. The other toys think that Woody has tossed RC from the moving van, but Lenny sees that the cowboy is actually riding the toy car.

Where's Woody?
When Woody gets mixed up in a yard sale after saving Wheezy, the gang uses Lenny to track him. He is able to give them a close-up of the toy-napper Al McWhiggin.

"He's lighting it! He's lighting it!"

Looking good
Lenny helps the other toys to stay informed about what's going on in the outside world. However, sometimes it's a tough job – when Andy lives next door to Sid, it is Lenny who has to tell the other toys about the gruesome experiments in Sid's yard.

Wind-up handle

Magnifying eyes

Movable feet

MULTITALENTED MIKE has a number of clever functions, including a built-in radio, tape player and microphone. He is a very useful toy to know! When he's not working, Mike likes to hang out with Mr Spell. They have electronics in common, after all.

Say it loud
When Woody needs to make his voice heard at toy meetings, he uses Mike's handy built-in microphone.

Mobile Mike

Mike's long, yellow cord allows Woody to walk and talk at the same time. Sometimes it's hard for Mike to keep up with wandering Woody!

Tape player buttons

Radio functions

Handle for easy carrying

Built-in microphone

Musical Mike

Mike is more than just Woody's mouthpiece – he has musical talents, too. Whenever the toys want to party, Mike provides the tunes. Wheezy is so pleased with his new squeaker that he bursts into song, and Mike is right there to help him out!

AM · · 54 60 · 80 100 130 160 x10kHz
FM 88 92 96 100 106 108 MHz

ON OFF

PLAYSKOOL

ALIENS

THE THREE-EYED green Aliens aren't actually from outer space – they're prizes in a game at the *Pizza Planet* restaurant. The squeaky toys all long to be chosen by the all-powerful metal Claw because they think it will lead them to a better place. For three lucky Aliens, that place is Andy's room!

Father figure

These three little Aliens were destined to spend their lives swinging from the rear-view mirror in a *Pizza Planet* truck, until Mr Potato Head rescued them. Now they call him "Daddy" and would follow him anywhere!

Life at Sunnyside

At first, the Aliens think that Sunnyside is great – there are plenty of claw toys. However, when the young kids arrive in the Caterpillar room, the Aliens suffer a serious squishing!

"We are eternally grateful."

Unlikely heroes

The Aliens' belief in the power of the Claw seems odd to the other toys in Andy's room. However, when the toys are about to be toasted in a trash incinerator, the little green guys know exactly how to save them – with a mechanical claw!

Rubber antenna

Pizza Planet logo

Rubber bodies

BUSTER

WHEN ANDY GETS a puppy for Christmas, Woody and Buzz just hope that they won't become chew toys. Fortunately, with Buster around, the only danger for the toys is having their parts or paint lovingly licked off, or occasionally being knocked over by the playful pup's wagging tail!

Decoy dog
Buster also has some useful acting skills. When Woody needs to get into the yard, he hangs on Buster's back while the talented dog "acts casual".

Old dog
Like his owner, Andy, Buster eventually grows up. Gone are the days when Buster could give Woody a wild ride around the house. He's barely able to roll over anymore.

Collar with name and address tag

Fun and games
One of Buster's favourite games is hide and seek. Woody hides while the rest of the gang try to hold Buster off. Buster then uses his canine nose to seek out his cowboy pal.

Wet nose

Long, wet tongue

House trained
Buster is one smart dog! Woody teaches him to sit up, reach for the sky, and even play dead. Buster also loves to roll over and be tickled. However, he only takes orders from Sheriff Woody. When Andy tries to train him, the clever canine just acts dumb.

ANDY DAVIS

EVERY TOY DESERVES a kid like Andy. Lively and enthusiastic, he has a vivid imagination and loves to play exciting games with his toys. With a few cardboard boxes and some crayons, Andy can create a Wild West town or a space port. Best of all, he treats his toys like pals.

"Now, you gotta promise to take good care of these guys."

Top team
As a little kid, Andy loves all his toys, but Woody and Buzz are his favourites. They are the stars of his games and the toys who sleep on his bed at night.

Cowboy kid
Every year, Andy goes to Cowboy Camp. He always takes his best pal Woody along for the ride. For Woody, it is a special treat to spend time with Andy, without all the other toys around.

All grown up
The toys watch Andy grow from a sweet little boy into a kind young man. As a grown-up, Andy drives a car, not a make-believe spaceship!

Serious expression

Laptop computer

Growing pains
Now Andy is old enough to go to college, he faces a tough decision about what to do with his toys. Although he hasn't played with them for a while, it is still hard to say goodbye.

MOLLY DAVIS

LIKE MOST LITTLE sisters, Molly has always wanted what her big brother has. First, it was his toys; now it is his bedroom. Molly often tried to play with Mr Potato Head and the rest of the gang, but she wasn't quite as gentle as her brother. When she was a baby, Molly had a tendency to dribble on the toys, so they nicknamed her "Princess Drool".

Princess Drool
For a while, Andy and Molly shared a room. Molly learned a lot about how to play with toys by watching her big brother, as soon as she was out of her drooling phase...

"Do I still get your room?"

Young lady
Molly likes to think she is as grown up as Andy, but she is still only 10 years old. She is more interested in video games, her MP3 player, her mobile phone, or reading magazines, rather than playing with toys.

Best brother
Andy and Molly have always been close. Molly will miss her big brother when he goes to college, but at least it means she gets his big bedroom!

MP3 player

No dolls!
Molly used to love playing with her Barbie doll, but she is way too grown up for that now. She is happy to donate her Barbie to Sunnyside so another child can play with her.

Fashionable outfit

19

ANDY'S NEIGHBOUR couldn't be more different than him: While Andy is a caring toy owner, Sid is every toy's worst nightmare! The mixed-up kid doesn't play with his toys; he experiments on them. He enjoys torturing toys and then blowing them up in his yard. No toy ever returns from Sid's house…

Super slob
Sid sleeps on a bare mattress with toy parts, mouldy snacks, toy-torturing tools and dirty clothes littering his filthy bedroom.

Playing with fire
All children know that they shouldn't play with matches, but Sid doesn't care. He loves matches, fireworks and pretty much anything that is dangerous or horrible!

Babyhead

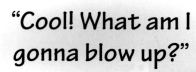

Scud
Sid's mean mutt Scud puts the "terror" in terrier. The horrible hound likes destroying toys as much as his master does.

"Cool! What am I gonna blow up?"

Payback
Like many bullies, underneath it all Sid is a complete coward. When Woody and the other toys break the rules and come to life in front of Sid, the creepy kid runs off screaming!

Scared expression

Skull t-shirt

HANNAH PHILLIPS

IT'S NOT EASY being Sid's little sister. Kind-hearted Hannah not only has to watch out for her big brother's bullying ways, but also her favourite toys keep not-so-mysteriously disappearing to become Sid's experiments. How would you like to find your favourite toy with a brand new head? Poor Hannah...

Poor Janie
Sid thinks that he has made Hannah's Janie doll "all better", but Hannah preferred her without a pterodactyl's head!

Toy tea party
Hannah always takes care of any disturbed toys she finds. After an encounter with Sid, Buzz finds comfort as Mrs Nesbit in one of Hannah's games.

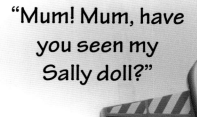

Did You Know?
Hannah eventually gets her revenge – when Sid runs screaming from his toys, Hannah chases him with her doll!

A cool head
Hannah is tougher than she looks. Her toys might be damaged, but she makes the best of a bad situation and hosts tea parties for all of her headless dolls.

"Mum! Mum, have you seen my Sally doll?"

Cute purple t-shirt

Broken toy

SID'S TOYS

THEY MIGHT LOOK frightening, but this mixed-up bunch is just as friendly as Andy's toys. Each mutant toy is the product of one of Sid's experiments. Pieces of different toys have been ripped apart and joined together to make strange new creations.

Misunderstanding
At first, Woody thinks that Babyhead and the mutant toys are as scary as Sid!

Fishing hook

Erector-set legs

Legs
Part doll, part fishing rod, Legs has a great combination of length and strength. She helps Sid fall hook, line and sinker for Woody's plan to save Buzz from Sid.

Babyhead
The leader of Sid's toys lives under Sid's bed. She taps Morse Code to let the other toys know when it's safe to come out of hiding.

Hand-in-the-Box
He looks monstrous, but this toy is always happy to lend a hand. He gets around by dragging himself across the floor.

Painted wooden box

Strong doll arms

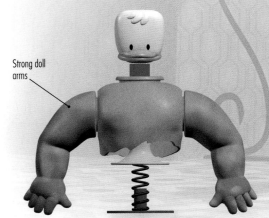

Ducky
This squeaky toy is the only one of the mutant toys that can make a noise. His unique body helps him spring into action to save fellow toys.

AL MCWHIGGIN

AL IS THE OWNER of *Al's Toy Barn*. This greedy grown-up doesn't like toys because they are fun to play with; he just likes them for the money he can make off of them. He is obsessed with collecting rare toys so he can sell them to museums and make a huge profit.

Anything for a buck!
Al will do anything he can to get customers to come to Al's Toy Barn. He'll even dress up as a chicken if it will make him some cash!

"You, my little cowboy friend, are gonna make me big buck-buck-bucks!"

Fake cheerfulness

Toynapper
The gang is able to track Woody to *Al's Toy Barn*, thanks to Al's personalised licence plate. They just have to crack the code first!

Big phony
On the outside, Al appears confident and in control, but inside he is a nervous wreck! When he toy-naps Woody from the yard sale, he finds that his stolen treasure is damaged and freaks out.

Did You Know?
Rumour has it that Al wasn't allowed to play with toys as a child, so he makes up for it as an adult by collecting them.

MR SPELL

MR SPELL IS a natural teacher. He taught Andy to spell, and also makes an effort to educate the other toys in Andy's room. Mr Spell runs a series of special awareness sessions for the toys on important subjects, such as the effects of plastic corrosion and what to do if you're swallowed!

Perfectly polite

Mr Spell gets around by shuffling clumsily from side to side, but his etiquette is perfect. When Woody thanks him for his help, he spells out "You're welcome".

Clever toy

Mr Spell is no action figure – he's built for educational purposes. But although he's a little square, the other toys respect him for his wide vocabulary and large memory.

Code breaker

When Woody is toy-napped, the gang knows that Al's licence plate is a clue. With Mr Spell's help, Buzz breaks the code.

Did You Know?

Mr Spell, Wheezy, Etch, Lenny, RC and Rocky are all believed to have been sold in the same yard sale.

Computer screen

Alphabetical keypad

THIS GOLD-DIGGING toy acts like a kindly old-timer, but if you dig a little deeper, the Prospector is actually devious and sneaky. The mint-condition meanie has never been taken out of his box, and he dreams of being in a museum. He has spent his life on a shelf and he likes it that way!

Mint-in-the-box

The Prospector is "mint-in-the-box" because he has never been played with or loved by a child. He can't understand why Jessie and Bullseye prefer life outside their packaging. He's a collectable, not a toy!

Detachable hat

Complete set
When Al McWhiggin buys Woody, the Prospector is delighted and will do anything he can to keep the gang together.

Did You Know?
In *Woody's Roundup*, the Prospector is nicknamed "Stinky Pete", but in the show he is accident prone rather than downright mean.

Neckerchief made from the same material as Woody's shirt

"No hand-me-down cowboy doll is gonna mess it up for me now."

Plastic pickaxe

Stinky Pete
When Woody decides his place is with Andy and the other toys, the Prospector shows his true colours. He breaks out of his box and does everything he can to stop Woody from leaving.

JESSIE

JESSIE THE yodelling cowgirl puts the "wild" into Wild West. The rough, tough tomboy loves to throw herself into adventures – once, she even jumped from a moving plane! Jessie is a fun-loving toy, but she has a deep fear of being abandoned or put into storage.

Hair made of red yarn

Authentic cowgirl belt buckle

"Yodel-ay-hee-hoo!"

Synthetic cow-hide chaps

Cowgirl boots

Soft side
Woody might be her Sheriff, but there is only one toy for Jessie – Buzz Lightyear. She thinks he is the cutest spaceman she has ever seen. Buzz is equally smitten with the kooky cowgirl but doesn't know how to show it, unless he is in Spanish mode…

Biggest fear
Jessie used to belong to a little girl named Emily, who loved her very much. However, when Emily grew up, she forgot about her favourite toy, and Jessie was eventually donated to charity.

Part of the gang
One of the happiest moments of Jessie's life was when she was reunited with Sheriff Woody and the *Roundup* gang was complete again. Finally getting out of her box and becoming a proper toy again was a dream come true.

Did You Know?
Jessie was shut away in storage for many years by toy collector Al McWhiggin, until Woody rescued her.

BULLSEYE

BULLSEYE WAS SHERIFF Woody's trusty steed in *Woody's Roundup*. This happy, hoof-kickin' horse is one of the most trusting and loyal creatures in the toy gang. He can't talk, but his big eyes and expressive body language say it all. Bullseye adores Woody and would do anything for his beloved Sheriff.

Big eyes

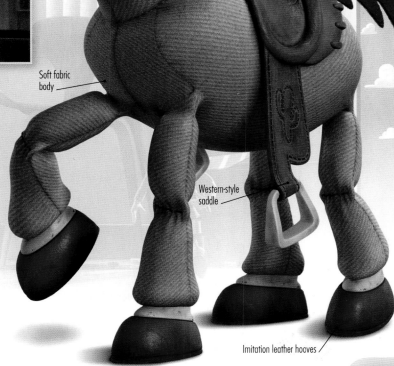

Horse heartbreak
When the toys end up at Sunnyside Daycare, Bullseye misses Sheriff Woody terribly.

Did You Know?
Andy printed a letter on the bottom of each of Bullseye's four hooves: A, N, D and Y. He is a real toy now!

Puppy love
With his big brown eyes, loyal nature and wagging tail, Bullseye is sometimes more like a giant puppy than a horse. When he is happy, he also loves to lick Woody!

Soft fabric body

Saddle up!
Bullseye specialises in helping Sheriff Woody save the day. However, he also has other talents: He puts his best hoof forward to switch on the video player, dim the lights in Andy's room and work the TV remote.

Western-style saddle

Imitation leather hooves

EMPEROR ZURG

EMPEROR ZURG IS Buzz Lightyear's archenemy. The evil Emperor from the planet Xrghthung has sworn to destroy Buzz and the Galactic Alliance. Freed from his box at *Al's Toy Barn*, Zurg attempts to take over the universe. Like Buzz, he has issues with being a "toy".

> "So, we meet again Buzz Lightyear, for the last time!"

Evil red eyes

Evil cape

Almost invincible purple armour

Dino defeat
Zurg is defeated by a surprising opponent – Rex. The timid tyrannosaurus thinks that Zurg is winning and can't bear to watch. As he turns away, Rex's clumsy tail sweeps Zurg off his feet. Game over!

Bad dad
As Zurg and New Buzz do battle, the evil emperor hits the space ranger with an unexpected blow: Zurg reveals he is actually Buzz's father! Against the odds, father and son start to bond.

NEW BUZZ

AT *AL'S TOY BARN*, Buzz Lightyear sees a whole aisle of new Buzz action figures. Thankfully, Buzz has come to terms with the fact that he's a toy and is impressed, not confused! However, Buzz is tempted by the new version's utility belt and tries to grab one.

Protective helmet

New model
Buzz can't resist the new utility belt, which has cool anti-gravity buttons and special climbing magnets!

Concealed space wings

Buzz #2
When New Buzz spots someone trying to steal his utility belt, he arrests him immediately! Trapping Buzz in his box, New Buzz sets off on an adventure with the rest of Andy's toys.

Super high-tech utility belt

Who's who?
The other toys think that Buzz is acting weird – he keeps talking about laser beams and booster pods. However, when the real Buzz shows up, they can't tell them apart – until they look under Buzz's space boot and find Andy's name.

THE CLEANER

KNOWN AS "the Cleaner", this mysterious old man repairs and restores old toys for Al. He can bring even the oldest of toys back to life with painstaking skill and a very steady hand. Using a minute dab of paint here, a tiny stitch there or even a new glass eyeball, the Cleaner creates miniature masterpieces.

Fixing Woody

The Cleaner not only fixes Woody, but he also retouches his cheeks, paints out a bald spot on his head and cleans his eyes and ears. His final touch is to paint out Andy's name on his boot.

"Ya can't rush art."

Sparse grey hair

Smartly dressed

On the case

The Cleaner carries everything he needs inside a specially adapted case. It has dozens of drawers containing paints, spare toy parts and even a toy treatment chair and bib.

Ancient artist

The Cleaner always concentrates completely on the job in hand and takes great pride in his work. He doesn't care what happens to the toys when he has finished with them; for him it is all about the craft.

Special case

Did You Know?

The Cleaner's real name is Geri. When he is not restoring toys, he likes to relax by playing chess in the park.

WHEEZY

EVER SINCE HIS squeaker broke, Wheezy has been languishing on Andy's bookshelf feeling sorry for himself. Andy's mum must have forgotten to get him fixed, and now he's gathered so much dust that he's become asthmatic! The pessimistic penguin is convinced he's destined for the next yard sale.

Reunited
Woody finds Wheezy behind some dusty books. The poor penguin is in low spirits and poor health. Woody tries to cheer him up before he notices that Wheezy is right – Andy's mum is about to have a yard sale!

"We're all just one stitch away from here..."

Sad expression

Red bow tie

Noble sacrifice
Woody saves Wheezy from the yard sale, but Woody gets sold instead – to toy collector Al McWhiggin.

Flightless wings

Karaoke king
When Wheezy finally gets his squeaker repaired, he is like a brand-new penguin. Penguins might not be able to fly, but this little guy certainly can sing. With a little help from Mike, he puts on a show for the other toys.

MRS DAVIS

MRS DAVIS IS a loving mum to Andy and Molly. She always seems to know just what they like – from great birthday parties and perfect presents to tasty treats at *Pizza Planet*. However, Mrs Davis is no pushover – she has rules. She expects Andy to be nice to his sister, pick up his toys and wash his hands occasionally!

Toy fear

Mrs Davis is a great mum to Andy, but his toys live in fear that she will either replace them or throw them out. Birthdays and Christmas are particularly stressful times for the toys.

"I'm sorry, honey, but you know... toys don't last forever."

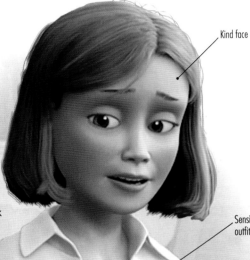

Kind face

Sensible outfit

Clearing out

When Mrs Davis sees a black bin bag, she doesn't hesitate in putting it out with the rest of the rubbish. She doesn't know that it is full of Andy's toys and that he had planned on keeping them!

No hoarding

Mrs Davis encourages her children to look forward and not hang on to too many of their toys. This means there have been plenty of yard sales and donations to places like Sunnyside Daycare over the years.

BONNIE

SWEET-NATURED BONNIE is everything a toy could hope for in an owner, even a toy who has previously been owned and loved by Andy. Kind, exuberant and with a colourful imagination, Bonnie makes life for her toys a lot of fun.

New owner

Andy is sad to part with his beloved toys, but he knows that giving them to Bonnie is the right thing for all of them. She will take care of them, and, most importantly, she will play with them.

Kindergarten nerves

Bonnie feels much braver with a friendly toy in her arms. She hopes to take one to kindergarten, but is told that it is not allowed.

Pink tutu

New toys

Bonnie is thrilled to introduce Andy's toys to her gang. More toys means more fun for everyone!

"We have a guest!"

Bandage

Toy rescuer

Unlike some kids at Sunnyside Daycare, Bonnie takes loving care of all toys – not just her own. She even rescues broken toys, including Woody when a trip on a kite leaves him hanging on a tree! Bonnie can be shy, and is rather nervous about starting kindergarten.

Yellow Wellington boots

BARBIE AND KEN

BARBIE AND KEN are Sunnyside's "it" couple. With their flawless hair, perfect plastic skin and impeccable physiques, they're always all dolled up. Even when things start to get tough, they stay picture-perfect.

Hench-doll
Underneath his stylish exterior, Ken has a dark secret – he works for Lotso. Ken runs Lotso's creepy casino inside the daycare vending machine.

Fashionable blue shirt

Perfect pair
When Barbie and Ken meet, it's love at first sight. They make each other happy and share a love of fashion – they are meant for each other!

Stylish striped leg warmers

New start
With Lotso gone, Barbie and the reformed Ken take over Sunnyside. Together, they make Sunnyside a happier place for toys to live.

Brainy beauty
Barbie is as smart as she is pretty. She might be in love with Ken, but when she realises what is truly going on at Sunnyside Daycare, she dumps him.

Did You Know?
Barbie makes Ken tell her about Lotso's plans by ripping up his beloved outfits one by one.

Cool, blue loafers

LOTSO

LOTSO LOOKS LOVABLE and huggable: He has a soft, plush body, a velvety purple nose and smells of strawberries. However, underneath his cuddly exterior, Lotso is a very bitter bear and rules Sunnyside Daycare through fear and intimidation. He causes Andy's toys Lotso trouble!

Toy terror
Andy's toys soon work out what Lotso is really like, but Buzz gets caught spying on him. Lotso tries to make the space toy join his gang, but Buzz refuses. So the gang resets Buzz...

Lotso pain
Lotso was once owned by a girl named Daisy, but she left him behind at a picnic. He found his way home, but Daisy had replaced him with another bear. Lotso came to Sunnyside to avoid the heartbreak of being owned and to take his hurt feelings out on other toys.

Not so nice
When Andy's toys arrive at Sunnyside, Lotso seems kind and welcoming, but it is all an act. Lotso makes sure that he and his cronies are comfortable, while new toys suffer!

Fake, charming smile

Cuddly body

Walking cane

"You've got a playdate with destiny!"

LOTSO'S GANG

LOTSO IS IN CONTROL at Sunnyside Daycare, but he needs a team of terrifying toys to do his bidding. Each member of Lotso's gang has a special talent that keeps the other toys in line so that their formidable leader can stay in power.

Play pal
Chunk's oversized, poseable legs make him an excellent toy for the kids at Sunnyside – when he's in friendly mode, that is.

Twitch
Life is easy for Twitch at Sunnyside. As one of Lotso's muscle-bound henchtoys, he is guaranteed first-class treatment in the workshop spa and his pick of the longlife batteries.

Battlestaff

Removable chest armour

Powerful wings

Mean face

Sparks
This robot is programmed to be a mean machine. Sparks has flashing red LED eyes and rolls around Sunnyside on his caterpillar tracks, carrying out Lotso's orders.

Sparks shoot from Sparks's chest – but they are completely safe for children!

Flashing red eyes

Painful pincers

Oversized limbs

Chunk
Chunk is covered in spikes and has massive fists ready to demolish anything in his way. The mean monster laughs when new arrivals at Sunnyside suffer – he has a heart of stone.

Stretch

With her glittery body and huge grin, Stretch looks like a fun-loving mollusc, but she is always ready to be the long arm of Lotso's laws. Made from a sticky substance that can withstand extreme stretching, the purple octopus uses her tentacles to capture any runaway toys.

Friendly face

Rubbery leg

Sticky suckers

Big Baby

This monstrous life-size baby doll is Lotso's right-hand toy. He makes sure that the other toys stick to Lotso's rules – or else! But Lotso lies to Big Baby for his own evil ends: Daisy did care about Big Baby all along.

Fake milk

Scribble tattoos

"It was filed under 'Lightyear.'"

The Bookworm

Growing up

Lotso pushes Big Baby too far by telling him that he is just a baby for still missing his owner, Daisy. Big Baby finally has enough – he dumps the selfish teddy in the dumpster and blows him a raspberry!

The Bookworm

The Bookworm looks like a harmless brainiac. However, this wiggly villain is the brains of Lotso's gang, maintaining a library of instruction manuals for every toy imaginable.

Crisp, white shirt

Bright, sturdy torch

CHATTER TELEPHONE has a permanently happy face, but this pull-along phone is way past his best. He is known as the "Lifer" at Sunnyside because he has been there so long. He has witnessed a long line of toys try – and fail – to escape. But Chatter is a tough telephone, and he won't let Sunnyside break him.

Phone-y smile
Chatter Telephone is always smiling on the outside, but inside he is sad and longs for the day when Sunnyside can be a happy place. When Lotso is ousted, Chatter's smile is finally real.

Time to talk
Chatter is the only toy who dares speak out about Lotso's reign at Sunnyside. He lets Woody know the best way to escape.

"I've been here years, they'll never break me."

Did You Know?
Telephones used to look just like Chatter. They had rotating dials instead of push buttons. Crazy!

Broken phone
Chatter might have seen better days, but he's a tough toy. Even when he is punished by Lotso's thugs for talking to Woody, he manages to pull through. They can break his receiver, but they can't break his spirit!

Eyes move up and down

Receiver

Rotating dial

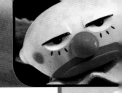

THIS SAD CLOWN has had a hard life. His owner, Daisy, accidentally left her favourite toys – Chuckles, Lotso and Big Baby – at a roadside stop. After that, poor Chuckles had to endure the Caterpillar room and Lotso's reign of terror at Sunnyside. However, sweet Bonnie took pity on his sad eyes and downturned mouth and gave him a new home.

Happy clown
Finally, Chuckles cracks a smile for the first time in years when he sees a drawing of himself by Bonnie.

Sad times
Chuckles sees nothing funny about the situation at Sunnyside and tells Woody some heart-breaking tales about his time there.

"We were lost, cast off, unloved, unwanted."

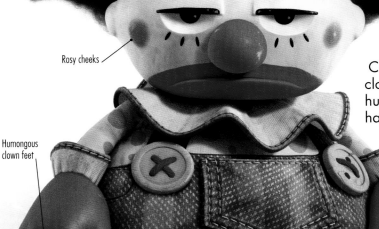

Rosy cheeks

Humongous clown feet

Clowning around
Chuckles has all the classic clown features: He's got huge clown feet, blue fuzzy hair, thick makeup and a red nose. The only thing missing is his smile, but now that he lives at Bonnie's, he's laughing – on the inside at least.

BUTTERCUP

BUTTERCUP IS A neatly groomed soft toy unicorn, with a majestic gold horn and fun-to-comb mane and tail. However, underneath his soft and sparkly exterior, this mythical horse is a straight-up, no-nonsense kind of toy who always tells it exactly like it is.

Mythical golden horn

Only kidding!
Buttercup likes to amuse his pals by playing jokes. When Woody arrives at Bonnie's, Buttercup warns him there is no way out! He's just horsing around, of course.

Fun-to-comb tail

Velvety soft fur

Good advice
Buttercup has plenty of acting advice for Woody to help him in Bonnie's role-playing games. Woody makes a promising debut, and he's not even classically trained!

"We do a lot of improv here... you'll be fine."

Buttercup's buddies
Buttercup might be gruff, but he is happy to make friends with Woody and the gang when they arrive at Bonnie's. He's delighted to have a four-legged friend in Bullseye but discovers that he has the most in common with the cynical porker, Hamm.

TRIXIE

TRIXIE IS BONNIE'S prehistoric playmate. Made from rigid, durable blue and purple plastic, Trixie is one dinosaur who's never going to be extinct, or even break. Like all of Bonnie's toys, she is an accomplished actor, and finds that creating a backstory helps her to understand her characters better.

Dino diva
Trixie is one talented Triceratops and always gives her very best in Bonnie's games. In her latest role, she has just come back from the doctor with life-changing news!

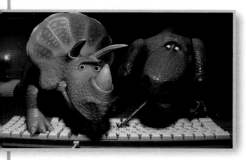

Prehistoric pals
Rex has always been worried about meeting another dino, but sweet-natured Trixie quickly puts him at ease. The dino duo become great friends and bond over their love of computer games.

"It's just a dinosaur!"

Computer nerd
Trixie is a techno-loving Triceratops. She spends a lot of time on the computer, swapping messages with her dinosaur buddy VelociSTAR237, who lives down the street.

Plastic horn

Movable legs

MR PRICKLEPANTS

PRICKLY BY NAME, prickly by nature, Mr Pricklepants is Bonnie's hedgehog toy. The lederhosen-wearing hedgehog is a dedicated actor and is happiest when he's on stage, delivering crowd-pleasing performances to the other toys.

True friend
Mr Pricklepants may be a little spiky, but he's actually a real softy. He even comes out of character – which is unheard of – to warn Woody that his friends aren't safe at Sunnyside.

Did You Know?
One of Mr Pricklepants's starring roles is Romeo alongside an Alien playing Juliet in one of Bonnie's games.

"Well, excuse me! I am trying to stay in character."

Quiet please
Mr Pricklepants takes his craft very seriously. It takes immense concentration to stay in character, and he has a habit of telling his fellow toys to "Shhh!", earning him the nickname "Baron von Shush".

Jaunty hat

Star toy
All of Bonnie's toys enjoy their daily improvisations, but no one more than Mr Pricklepants. He just always seems to hog the limelight.

DOLLY

DOLLY IS BONNIE'S stuffed rag doll. With her big eyes, sweet smile and butterfly clips in her hair, she is as cute as the buttons on her orange, polka-dot dress. But for some reason, Dolly is often cast as the villain in Bonnie's roleplays. Maybe it's time she got herself an agent!

First impressions
Dolly is happy to welcome any new additions to Bonnie's room and is always willing to impart sound advice to her fellow toys.

Happy family
With Andy's toys joining the gang, Dolly looks forward to many happy days acting in Bonnie's plays. Maybe one of the new toys can play the villain instead!

"Wow, cowboy. You just jump right in, don't you?"

Did You Know?
Dolly makes Chuckles smile for the first time since he was abandoned – by showing him Bonnie's drawing of him smiling.

Down-to-earth doll
On her first meeting with Woody, Dolly suggests he should change his name to something more interesting to succeed in the crazy world of show business. She certainly wishes she had a better stage name than plain old "Dolly".

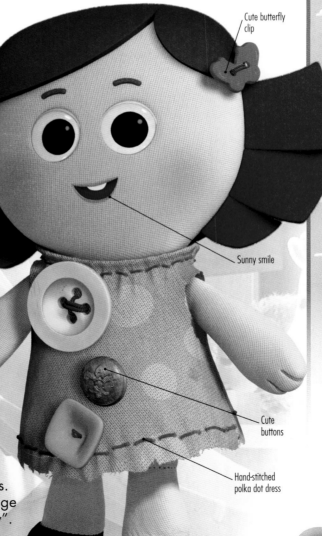

Cute butterfly clip

Sunny smile

Cute buttons

Hand-stitched polka dot dress

GABBY GABBY

THIS PRETTY 1950s doll longs to ask a kid to be her friend. But she can't – a faulty voice box means her words come out all garbled. Gabby Gabby still dreams of one day finding a voice... and a kid. Until then, she sits forgotten in a cabinet in the Second Chance Antiques store, with only her dummy friends for company.

Cute bunches

Sweet smile

Night patrol
Each night, Gabby Gabby patrols the aisles in an old, squeaky baby carriage pushed by Benson, her assistant. Gabby Gabby is excited to meet Woody, who is exploring the store. She's even more excited when she spots Woody's voice pull cord.

Dummies
Benson is a ventriloquist's dummy who silently accompanies Gabby Gabby everywhere. His head turns 360 degrees, giving him a very creepy look. Gabby Gabby has three other dummy helpers, but Benson is easy to pick out by his red bow tie.

Yellow cotton dress

Harmony
Gabby Gabby is devoted to Harmony, the store owner's little granddaughter. She watches Harmony's games, wishing she could be a part of them. When Harmony plays "teatime" with her tea set, Gabby Gabby silently copies her every move, lifting an invisible cup to her lips.

Did You Know?
Gabby Gabby's voice box is a tiny record player set into a compartment in her back.

Dainty yellow shoes

FORKY

FORKY IS MORE than a plastic spork – to Bonnie, he's the best toy in the world. After he helps her through a tough day at kindergarten, Bonnie refuses to be parted from Forky, even sleeping with him in her hand. Sadly, the stunned spork doesn't understand he's a toy, and keeps trying to hop into a bin.

Shocked spork
One minute, Forky is a used utensil snoozing happily in a nice warm bin. The next, he's a googly-eyed toy being fussed over by an excited little girl. It's enough to put his prongs in a spin!

Googly eyes

Lopsided smile

Making a friend
When a kid at kindergarten swipes Bonnie's craft supplies, Woody retrieves them from the bin but scoops up a plastic spork as well. Two pipe-cleaner arms, popsicle stick feet and a pair of googly eyes later, Bonnie has a new friend – Forky!

Did You Know?
Forky was expecting to be used just once – for soup, salad or chili – then thrown away.

Pipe-cleaner arms

Plastic pal
Woody cares a lot for Bonnie. It breaks his heart to see Forky always trying to escape from her. Woody makes it his job to toy-sit Forky until he can convince his plastic pal how important he is.

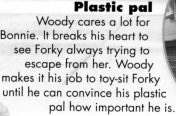

Popsicle stick feet

AT JUST HALF an inch tall, Giggle isn't exactly the long arm of the law. This pocket detective lives in a police badge, drives a tiny car and rides around on Bo's shoulder. Despite her size, Giggle has a big impact, tracking down lost animals with the Pet Patrol. She's funny, feisty and never runs out of energy.

Bo's backup
Giggle often rides with Bo, dishing out advice as well as practical assistance. Never a toy to mince her words, Giggle doesn't hold back with her opinions. If she meets a bozo, that's exactly what she'll call them.

—————— Miniature police hat

Pet Patrol
From her cosy badge home, Giggle runs Pet Patrol like a well-oiled machine. First, she studies her lost pets chart. Next, she pieces together clues. Then off she goes, picking up pooches, collecting cats and hunting down hamsters with smooth efficiency.

Tiny tie —

Small wonder
Being the size of a cricket can be a big advantage to a detective. Not many sleuths can hide under a fallen leaf, or conceal themselves in the shadow of a plastic cup.

Sensible shoes ——————

DUKE CABOOM

HE LEAPS! He spins! He balances! He's Duke Caboom – Canada's greatest motorcycle daredevil! Duke can do all these amazing things, but sadly, he couldn't win the love of a kid. When he was unboxed, Duke's kid discarded him because he wasn't as exciting as the TV commercial suggested. For all his swagger, Duke still feels the hurt.

Motorcycle hero
With his twirling moustache, maple leaf cape and polished helmet, Duke looks every inch the hero. His winning smile and well-practiced triumphant poses are guaranteed to impress. Hopefully, his motorcycle skills are still up to scratch.

— Maple leaf belt buckle

Disappointing Duke
The TV commercial showed Duke and his cycle whizzing effortlessly through a ring of fire and landing with a dash. The reality was different, as Duke's kid, Rejean, discovered. Duke came up short, and soon found himself thrown out with the Christmas rubbish.

Confidence boost
Bo needs Duke's help for a daring rescue jump, so she gives him a pep talk. His confidence boosted, Duke is back on his cycle in moments. When Bo asks if he can make the leap, Duke replies, "Yes I Canada!"

— Sleek motorcycle

Did You Know?
Duke may be a larger-than-life personality, but physically he is only half Woody's size.

DUCKY AND BUNNY

STUFFED TOYS Ducky and Bunny are prizes in a carnival game. For three long years, they've spent each day the same way – tied to the wall of prizes, waiting for a child to win them. Well, it might still happen! The squabbling stuffies bicker and argue constantly, but they can't be parted. That's because their wing and paw are firmly stitched together.

Fluffy ears

Hanging out
Ducky and Bunny are furious when Buzz joins them on the wall of prizes. The snazzy space ranger has taken the top prize spot – their spot. Together, they swing wildly, hoping to kick Buzz into oblivion.

Bunny
For a toy with such big ears, Bunny isn't very good at listening, or at least listening to Ducky. Nevertheless, the wrangling rabbit is always there by Ducky's side when the going gets tough. Thanks to their stitching, he has to be.

Tiny legs

Did You Know?
Ducky and Bunny become Ducky and stucky when they try to follow Buzz through a narrow gap!

Ducky
This fluffy yellow duck toy has a small body but a big voice – and he likes to use it. Ducky is always nagging Bunny, especially when Bunny doesn't notice he needs help with reaching something. He can be rather sensitive about his tiny legs!

COMBAT CARL JRS.

HUT! HUT! HUT! The three Combat Carl Jrs. travel as a unit. They move from area to area, treating each playtime like a military manoeuvre. Combat Carl, Volcano Attack Combat Carl and Ice Attack Combat Carl love the outdoor life and rough play. Nothing beats the freedom of being lost toys – ownerless toys who can be played with by any kid who finds them.

Combat wear
The Carls were made in the same factory from the same mould. Just their clothing varies. Volcano Combat Carl is dressed for extreme heat conditions and Ice Combat Carl is decked out for the cold. Only the original Combat Carl wears traditional fatigues.

Fiery red gear

Snow goggles

Did You Know?
Whenever the Carls take turns to high-five someone, Ice Combat Carl is always left hanging.

Camouflage trousers

FLIK

WITH HIS BRIGHT ideas and wacky inventions, Flik is no ordinary ant. But somehow his clever schemes always end in disaster. Tired of slaving for Hopper and his greedy grasshopper gang, Flik steps up to help his colony. He is especially eager to help Princess Atta, who he adores. However, things don't go according to plan...

Did You Know?

Ants have the largest brains of any insect. Each ant brain has an amazing 250,000 brain cells, and the processing power of a small computer.

Hopeless harvester

Flik builds a grain-gathering gizmo, but it turns out to be a grain-spilling gadget instead! Fortunately, Flik never gives up and soon has a new idea.

Head full of bright ideas

"I was just trying to help."

Spindly legs

Big city: here I come!

Flik is not only inventive, he's also brave. He has the courage to leave Ant Island and go to the city in search of bigger bugs to defend the colony.

Brainy and brave

Flik convinces a troupe of circus bugs to help the ants and comes up with several plans to defeat the grasshoppers. However, when all the plans fail, Flik puts himself in danger to defeat Hopper. Flik's bravery inspires the other ants to be more gutsy, too.

Victory fireworks!

With Hopper defeated, the ants say farewell to the circus bugs by firing grains into the air. It turns out Flik's grain-gathering gizmo does have a use after all!

ATTA

A BORN WORRIER, Princess Atta has a way to go before she is ready to be queen of the colony. In fact, Atta feels totally antsy about the possibility of messing up royally and thinks that Flik is just making her job harder. Her heart is in the right place, though, and she just wants what's best for her subjects.

Mother and daughter
Although her mother is on hand for advice, it is time for Atta to make her own decisions. She has to prove that she has what it takes to wear the Queen's crown.

Princess crown made from leaves

Pretty wings

A bug's love
Relieved that the colony is finally safe from the grasshoppers, Atta plants a big kiss on Flik's cheek. It's a dream come true for Flik, and Atta finally realises that he is the bug for her.

Elegant pose

Learning to lead
As a queen-ant-in-training, Atta takes her responsibilities very seriously – maybe too seriously. Her mother, the Queen, wants her to loosen up. In the end, though, it's Flik's brave example that helps Atta to become a true leader.

"The ants pick the food, the ants keep the food and the grasshoppers leave!"

DOT

THANKS TO HER tiny name and tiny size, Princess Dot gets teased a lot. She's the smallest member of the Blueberry Scout Troop and the other kids call her "Your Royal Shortness". Luckily, Dot's not short on determination. The little princess has faith in Flik and helps him to believe in himself just when he's ready to give up.

Seeds of change
Flik tells Dot not to worry about being small – tiny seeds grow into giant trees. Later, Dot repeats these words to inspire Flik to return to Ant Island.

"It's payback time, Blueberry style!"

Small but fully grown wings

High flyer
Dot's big frustration is not being able to fly. When she has to bring Flik back to the colony, however, her determination to fly finally takes her up, up and away!

Fists closed in determination

Did You Know?
Little Dot is almost eaten by a bird, but Flik and the circus bugs save her! The little princess is a precious member of the colony.

Loyal fan
Dot thinks that Flik is the greatest, and that his inventions are super cool. In Dot's eyes, Flik can do no wrong, and her faith in him proves to be 100% on the dot! When Dot's big sister becomes Queen, the little ant inherits her princess tiara.

Short legs

QUEEN

THE QUEEN IS a sensible ruler and a kind, reassuring mother to Atta and Dot. She is also as tough as nails. Although the Queen is loyal to the old ways, she is willing to try Flik's ideas, as long as they don't put the colony in danger.

Old softy
The Queen never goes anywhere without Aphie, her cute little pet aphid. Maybe being a pet owner is what makes her so relaxed. She certainly loves to spoil Aphie, who adores her and laughs at all her jokes.

Queen's speech
Whether she's welcoming the circus bugs or thanking Flik, the Queen always has just the right words to say.

Elaborate flower crown

"Well, my boy, you came through."

A royal wave

Did You Know?
The Queen helps the circus bugs to trick Hopper by taking part in one of Manny's vanishing tricks!

Royal joker
The Queen has a good sense of humour and a practical view of life. She tells Atta how the grasshoppers come, eat and then leave. That, she believes, is the ants' lot in life. However, Flik shows her that things can change.

HOPPER

GANG LEADER HOPPER is as mean as they come. With a thick exoskeleton that creaks and rattles like armour, and spiny legs and feet, this big bully towers over the ants. However, Hopper has one major flaw – believing that he is smarter than everyone else.

Did You Know?
Hopper is tough, but there is one thing guaranteed to get his exoskeleton shaking with fright – birds!

Hopping mad
Every fall, Hopper and his gang demand an offering from the ants. Thanks to Flik, the ants have no food this year, so the nasty grasshoppers invade the ant hill instead.

Hopper towers over the tiny ants

"It's not about food, it's about keeping those ants in line."

A bug-eat-bug world
Hopper acts tough, but he knows that if the ants ever find out that they outnumber the grasshoppers, they will realise that they don't have to obey them. Hopper does everything in his power to keep the colony afraid of him. He demands that the ants gather up twice as much food before the next leaf falls, or "someone could get hurt".

Bird food
Flik tries to scare Hopper with a fake bird, but the plan fails. So, when Flik leads him to the nest of a real bird, Hopper thinks it's another trick – until it's too late.

MOLT

SOMETIMES IT'S hard to believe that Molt is Hopper's brother. Hopper always thinks before he speaks, but Molt's mouth doesn't seem to be connected to his brain at all (if he has one, that is). Molt never knows when to shut up, and he can be swayed into thinking just about anything.

Mummy's boy
Hopper admits he would have killed Molt long ago, if not for a promise he made to their mother on her deathbed.

"He's quite the motivational speaker, isn't he?"

Bungling brother
Molt's always getting into trouble. His foolish chatter even reveals Hopper's fear of birds to all the ants. He might be stupid, but at least Molt survives to get a job with the circus, while Hopper becomes bird food!

Whoops...
Even flying up and away like the other grasshoppers poses problems for Molt – the clumsy clod hits the ceiling!

Molt's skin is always flaking off

Did You Know?
Molt makes a fresh start by joining P.T. Flea's circus as a strongman. He even gets a new nickname – Tiny!

Strong arms

FRANCIS

TOUGH-TALKING Francis may be a ladybird, but he is no lady! Unfortunately, his beautiful big eyes and pretty wing cases give many circus-goers the wrong idea. Anyone who mistakes this hot-tempered clown for a girl is in for trouble, though.

Stick it to 'em
Francis is devoted to his friend Slim and, as the stick insect cannot fly, carries him on long journeys.

Den mother
Francis finds that he loves spending time with the young ants of Blueberry Troop. He even teaches them how to gamble!

Antenna

Did You Know?
Francis used to play a flower in P.T. Flea's circus, but this didn't last long – two flies flirting with him quickly put an end to his budding career!

Francis has a fierce temper!

Polka dot wings

"We are the greatest warriors in all Bugdom!"

Tough talker
In the big city, Francis is ready to fight anyone who suggests he's girlie, but on Ant Island, he gets in touch with his feminine side. When the Blueberry Troop make him an honorary den mother, Francis finally learns that having a soft spot doesn't make him a softie.

HEIMLICH

HEIMLICH IS A mighty munching machine with a big appetite and a big dream – to become a beautiful butterfly. But when Heimlich finally does get his wings, they are too stubby to support his great bulk! Fortunately, happy Heimlich is too easygoing to let that bother him for long.

Fast food
Heimlich never misses an opportunity to devour a quick meal. On the way to the ant colony, he sneaks in some in-flight snacks.

Heave
It doesn't really matter if Heimlich cannot fly. He has loyal friends to help him along the way.

Cheeks full of yummy food

"Bottle all gone. Baby wants pie!"

Hand holding yummy food

Belly full of yummy food

Worm on a stick
Heimlich doesn't only spend his time munching and clowning around. He can be brave and loyal, too. He lets Francis and Dot use him as bait to tempt an attacking bird away, and he plays his part in standing up to the grasshoppers.

MANNY

MYSTICAL MANNY'S magic show is the high point of P.T. Flea's Circus. The praying mantis takes his art, and himself, very seriously. With his British accent and dramatic gestures, Manny considers himself to be a true *artiste*.

山珍

Insectus transforminus!
Manny's performance includes a transformation act using the Chinese Cabinet of Metamorphosis (a takeaway box). It's a crowd-pleaser every time.

Large eyes

Two pairs of wings

Magic hands

Crystal balls
Manny and Gypsy's circus skills include pretending to see into the future.

"Yet again it is up to me to rescue the performance."

Kind words
For all his seriousness, deep down Manny is a gentle soul. He finds the right words to soothe Flik when he feels low: "I've made a living out of being a failure", Manny tells Flik. "And you sir – are NOT a failure!"

GYPSY

GYPSY IS MANNY'S wife and his assistant in the circus magic show. When she opens up her gorgeous wings, Gypsy is a real showstopper! However, she is usually happy to stand back and let her husband, Manny, take centre stage.

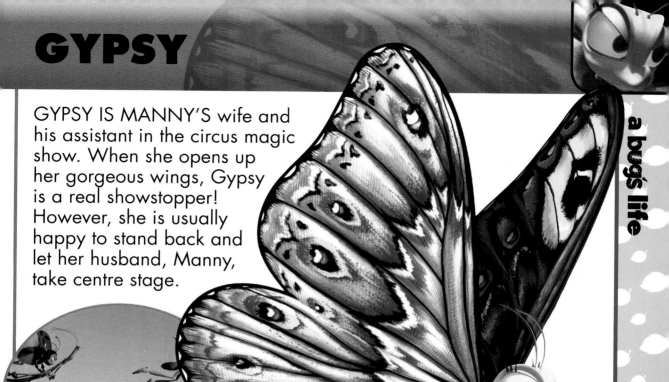

Colourful wings

Upturned nose

Off to Ant Island!
Gypsy is like a mother to the circus troupe. She often acts as their spokesbug.

"Shh! He's in a trance."

Slender legs

Amazing moth
Gypsy may look delicate, but she's not just lovely, she's brave, too. She flies in and flashes her wings to distract the creek bird when it is attacking Heimlich. And she refuses to tell Hopper how she and Manny have "magicked away" the Queen during their transformation act.

Did You Know?
Female gypsy moths are usually bigger than males, but many of them cannot fly.

Wise wife
Gypsy works hard helping Manny outside the circus ring as well as in it. Manny's head is so far up in the clouds, there's no telling how he'd ever manage without Gypsy's sensible guidance.

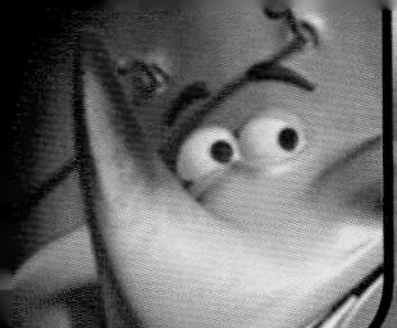

DIM

FLIK'S FIRST SIGHT of Dim, the rhinoceros beetle, leaves him in no doubt that he's found a troupe of truly tough bugs. But despite his scary-looking horn and thundering size, Dim is a total sweetie who wouldn't hurt a fly.

Super-strong wings

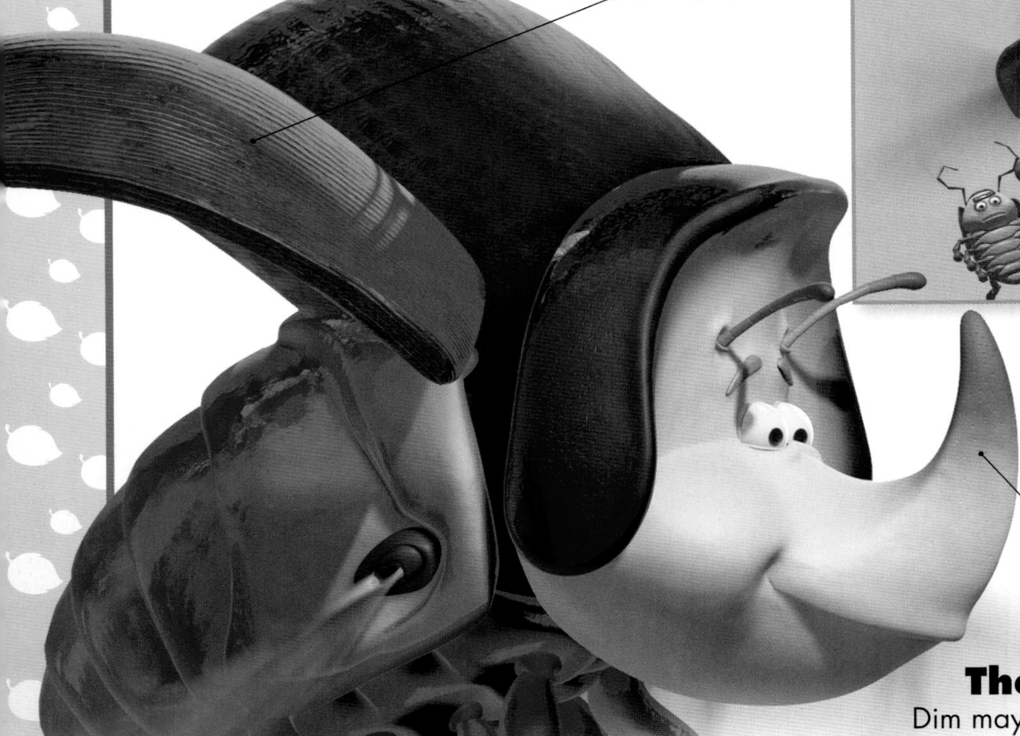

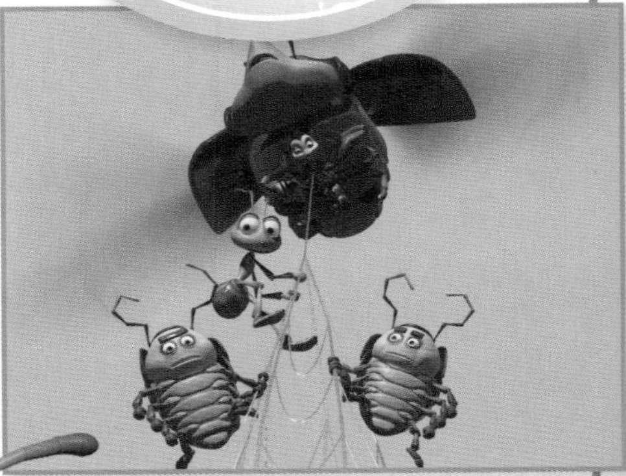

Safe flight
Dim's superior wing power allows him to airlift Dot, Tuck and Roll out of danger during the bird attack.

Large horn

The bugmobile
Dim may not be the brainiest bug, but he is dependable. His strength and size mean he also acts as the troupe's transportation. On Ant Island, he makes himself useful and popular by giving the young ants rides.

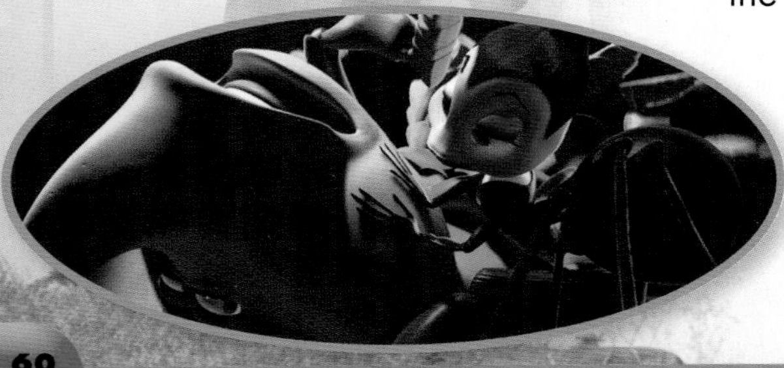

Tender trainer
Rosie is Dim's trainer, but sometimes she is more like a mother to him. She looks after Dim and soothes him when he's hurt.

"Dim don't wanna go."

TUCK AND ROLL

NO INSECT CAN match this pair of crazy pill bugs when it comes to acrobatics and gymnastic feats. Tuck and Roll spend all their time tucking, rolling, somersaulting, flipping and tumbling with tremendous zest.

Ta-da!
Tuck and Roll act as cannonballs in P.T. Flea's circus troupe. With their crooked smiles and waving legs, the pill bug pair end each routine with a flourish.

"You fired! You fired!"

Did You Know?
Tuck pulls off one of Hopper's antennas and uses it in the troupe's final show!

Tuck wears a slightly crazed expression

Baffled bugs
Tuck and Roll are from Hungary. Flik talks to them nonstop all the way to Ant Island, without realising that they don't understand a word of English.

Roll has a monobrow

Hopper's antenna

Pill bugs have eight legs

Tough twins
Tuck and Roll are a hot-tempered duo. They are always arguing and hitting each other. To onlookers, their squeaky squabbling is more entertaining than their tumbling. Even Hopper thinks it's funny.

P.T. FLEA

GREEDY CIRCUS owner and ringmaster P.T. Flea will do anything for money, including getting burned alive in the name of entertainment! The fiery flea spends most of his time yelling at his troupe, as they lurch from one disaster to another. Finally, he fires them!

Flea finale
The circus's "Flaming Death" finale begins with P.T. holding a lit match. It ends with his body being burned to a crisp. The audience loves it!

"They're gonna make me rich."

Ka-ching!
With a surprise hit on his hands, P.T. Flea tracks down the troupe and tries to win them back.

Greedy eyes

Did You Know?
P.T. Flea returns from the ant colony with a bigger and better circus, now including a troupe of acrobatic ants!

Money-hungry mouth

Money grabber
P.T. Flea is a parasite who squeezes money out of the low-lifes that visit his big top. If audiences complain that the show stinks, P.T.'s answer is simple: "No refunds after two minutes". His dream is to make the circus a moneymaking success.

Singed legs

Flammable body

THUMPER

SNARLING THUMPER is less like a grasshopper and more like a mad guard dog. When Hopper doesn't get his way, he uses Thumper as a threat. Vicious and unpredictable, Thumper has to be kept on a leash – and even then, it takes two handlers to control him!

a bug's life

Mean eyes

Menacing expression

Bad grasshopper!

Scary Thumper enjoys nothing more than terrifying others. But when the tables are turned, he reveals himself to be a complete coward. A smack from Dot and a roar from Dim is all it takes to make Thumper go from ferocious to frightened to fleeing in seconds!

Fierce hands

Size isn't everything

When the ants try to chase the grasshoppers away, Dot runs into Thumper. But the tough grasshopper gets more than he bargained for when he takes on determined Dot!

Mighty muscle

Wherever Hopper is, Thumper isn't far behind, ready to do some damage.

"Screech! Screech! Screech!"

SLIM

SARCASTIC AND A bit pessimistic, stick insect Slim has a fragile ego that is easily broken when people laugh at him. The problem is that he's a clown, so when an audience is laughing, it means that he has done a good job!

Stuck for words
Slim thinks he has star quality, but he is usually cast as a broom, a stick or a flower. Performing a "Spring flowers" routine with Francis is not his idea of show business!

> "Francis, you're making the maggots cry."

Long, sticklike head

Long, sticklike body

A way out!
Slim is quick to accept Flik's offer to travel to Ant Island. He thinks it will be the perfect escape from a group of flies who are after Francis.

Long, sticklike fingers

A friend indeed
Although he hates being laughed at, Slim reckons there's one good thing about being a clown – his fellow clowns. He's especially close to the tough ladybird, Francis, who carries Slim around by tucking him under a wing.

ROSIE

BLACK WIDOW spider Rosie is glamorous, talented and hardworking. At the circus, she is mistress of the high wire and Dim's trainer. Rosie is a real team player and is always ready to help out the rest of the troupe.

Misunderstanding
Like the rest of the troupe, at first Rosie doesn't understand what Flik is asking of them. She thinks he's a talent scout!

"Come on everyone. Break a leg!"

Spider skills
Rosie can weave a web so fast it makes your head spin – a skill that's useful when rescuing her friends from sticky situations. She can cast out a lifesaving line in record time – or use her silken thread to tie up an annoying busybody, such as P.T. Flea.

Rosie's role
In the "Flaming death" routine, Rosie's job is to spin the line that will save Tuck and Roll.

Stylish purple eyeshadow

Kind expression

Eight long legs

65

SULLEY

JAMES P. SULLIVAN, or Sulley, is the top Scarer at Monsters, Inc., a company that provides energy to Monstropolis by capturing the screams of children from the human world. Sulley is fierce on the Scare Floor, but off it, he's as friendly as he is furry.

Shaggy green and purple fur

Dream team

As new Scare Students at Monsters University, it seems that Sulley and Mike are too different to be friends at first. But they soon become extremely close. Now, these best pals live together, work together and hardly ever argue!

"May the best monster win."

New pal

Monsters believe that human kids are highly dangerous. At first, Sulley is scared of Boo. But he soon grows fond of her and finds a new way to power Monstropolis without scaring anyone – using children's laughter!

Modest monster

Sulley is an A-list celebrity around Monstropolis, but he doesn't let fame go to his furry head. Sulley treats everybody the same, whether they're co-workers or monsters. He's just a regular guy!

MIKE

FAST-LIVING AND FUN-LOVING, Mike is Sulley's Scare Assistant and best pal. He is a real ball of energy. You won't find Mike staying in and watching TV – unless it's to see himself in the new Monsters, Inc. commercial.

Monster love
Mike and his "Shmoopsie Poo" Celia only have an eye for each other. He treats her to dinner on her birthday and supplies her with an endless stream of compliments, which she loves.

Take the mike, Mike
When Monsters, Inc. changes from scaring kids to making them laugh, Mike puts his comedic skills to the test. Mike even resorts to swallowing his mic to make a child laugh. His jokes definitely need a little more work...

Monsters, Inc. hard hat

"Nothing is more important than our friendship."

Round body

Roar Recruit
Mike has plenty of skills to make up for the fact that he looks about as monstrous as a tennis ball. He is a quick learner and can bring out the best in those around him. Once he teams up with Sully at Monsters University, he becomes part of an unstoppable team.

Did You Know?
Mike has always suffered from poor eyesight. He gets his lenses from the upmarket Cyclops Optical. Well, when you've just got one eye, only the best will do!

RANDALL BOGGS

RANDALL BOGGS IS slimy, slippery and disgusting – and that's just his personality. The meanest monster around, he's Sulley's main rival at Monsters, Inc. Randall is challenging Sulley for the position of top Scarer, but one thing's for sure – he'll never win any popularity prizes!

Crafty expression

Secret plan
Randall has created a top secret scream-extracting machine and he plans to test it on a human child. But until he finds one, Mike the monster will have to do!

Lots of teeth

Total transformation
Randall wasn't always a sneaky scarer. When Mike first meets Randy at Monsters University, he is shy, nervous and sweet-natured. Randy admires his roommate's great determination.

Sneaky hand gesture

On the prowl
Repugnant Randall is a colour-changing chameleon who can make himself almost invisible. The creep then creeps around scaring children and annoying his rival monsters.

Lizard skin

MRS NESBITT

MRS NESBITT IS probably the least scary monster at Monsters, Inc. She runs the Monsters, Inc. school for young monsters with a perfect balance of firmness and understanding. Having four arms means the plump, purple-spotted monster can easily comfort more than one child at a time.

All monsters allowed
Mrs Nesbitt welcomes all monsters in her class. However, she might want to take a closer look at the purple "monster" with the eyes on stalks...

Teacher's pets
All the mini monsters love Mrs Nesbitt. Although they can misbehave sometimes, they think she's a class act and the perfect teacher to keep an eye on them... although her eyesight might need to be tested!

> ### Did You Know?
> Mrs Nesbitt has worked at Monsters, Inc. as a teacher since the company first opened.

Sensible hairstyle

Squishy body perfect for giving monster hugs

CELIA

AS THE RECEPTIONIST at Monsters, Inc., Celia has learned to be super-efficient. She has to greet visitors, answer the phones and make announcements over the intercom – sometimes all at the same time! It's a pity the five snakes on her head can't help her out.

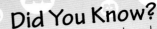
Purple snake-hair

Fashionable fur collar

Scaly shift dress

Mad monster

When Celia and the five snakes on her head get mad, Monstropolis had better watch out! Seeing that her Googly Bear – Mike – and Sulley are trying to escape from Randall, she makes sure she stops the horrible monster from catching them.

"Oh, Googly-woogly, you remembered!"

Long, elegant tentacles

True love

Celia and Mike are a match made in monster heaven. Although Mike sometimes makes her mad, she wouldn't change a thing about him.

Concise Celia

Celia has a no-nonsense approach in and out of the office. Although she loves a romantic night out with the apple of her eye, Mike, Celia keeps him on his six toes. If she senses that he is keeping secrets from her, she demands to know the truth – immediately!

ROZ

DISPATCH MANAGER FOR Scare Floor F, Roz is a stickler for the rules. Just one dirty look from this stern-looking giant slug is enough to make all the Scare Assistants tremble with fear, particularly if they haven't handed in their paperwork on time.

Permanent scowl

Sharp-eyed slug

This sly slug is bossy and conscientious for a reason! As leader of the CDA (Child Detection Agency), she worked undercover at Monsters, Inc. to expose the scandal at the company.

No sweet talking here!

Roz is immune to sweet talk – no matter how hard the assistants try, they just can't shift her permanent frown. There's more to Roz than scowls and sarcasm, however, and she always seems to know exactly what's going on at Monsters, Inc....

"I'm watching you Wazowski, always watching."

Slimy slug body

71

BOO

BOO IS ONLY two years old, but she is very brave. The plucky youngster is not afraid to hang out with a bunch of the weirdest-looking oddballs you can find. Boo has a limited vocabulary of about three words, but she has loads of energy and laughs at the most unexpected things, including her monster friends!

No more tears
Boo has a massive effect on Sulley and all of Monstropolis. Thanks to her influence, laughter rather than screams now fuel the city.

"Boo!"

Fake hair

Monster disguise
When Boo gets lost in the Monsters, Inc. factory, she tags along with a group of young monsters being shown around the factory. Her monster costume helps her to blend right in.

Plastic tentacles

Did You Know?
One of Boo's favourite toys is her Yodelling Jessie Cowgirl doll.

Here Kitty, Kitty
Boo is a very curious child and loves to go exploring. This causes some stress for Sulley, her favourite monster and friend. Boo thinks he looks like a giant pussycat and calls him "Kitty".

WATERNOOSE

PROUD, PROPER AND pretty
scary, Henry J. Waternoose
is the boss of Monsters, Inc.
The company has been in the
Waternoose family for three
generations, and Henry J. began his
illustrious career on the Scare Floor
when he was a young monster
(a long time ago).

Star pupil
Waternoose is proud of his top Scarer, Sulley,
and often uses his super scare skills to show
other monsters how it's done.

Horrible Henry
Waternoose pretends to
take care of Boo, but
really he is planning to
extract screams from her
with the horrible scream
extracting machine!

*"I'll kidnap a thousand
children before I let
this company die!"*

Fake friend
Underneath his professional exterior,
Waternoose is actually dishonest and
devious. He is facing a looming
scream shortage and is under
intense pressure to get his
employees to collect more
screams. He will do
anything to make
his company
profitable again,
even if it means
betraying loyal
friends like
Sulley.

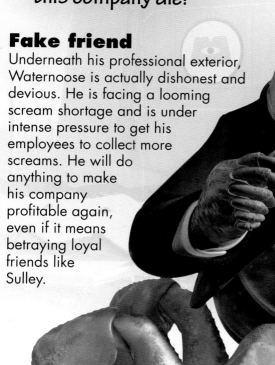

Smart tuxedo

Crablike legs

GEORGE

MONSTERS, INC.

GEORGE IS ONE of the most laid-back monsters on the Scare Floor. Easygoing and popular, he isn't too bothered about being the best. George would much rather take it easy with the other Scarers and share a joke or two on the Scare Floor than be at the top of the Scarer Leaderboard.

Contamination
Trouble seems to follow poor George everywhere. When a kid's sock gets stuck to his furry back, the CDA is called immediately to catch the contaminated monster. George has a very close shave and loses most of his shaggy fur!

Mild monster
Some might say that George is a little too carefree and, consequently, this accident-prone monster often gets into scrapes. George is good friends with Mike and Sulley, and they often hang out together on the Scare Floor.

George's horn

Did You Know?
At Monsters University, George was a member of the JOX fraternity. They were the snarliest students on campus!

Big, baby-blue eyes

Tufts of fur

Cone to stop George from scratching his freshly shaved skin

CLAWS

PETE "CLAWS" WARD has the largest, sharpest claws on the Scare Floor, and he's proud of it! Each morning, Claws lovingly extends his talons to their full, terrifying length, ready for a great day of scaring.

Dinnertime
After a hard day's work on the Scare Floor, Claws enjoys nothing more than getting his claws into a bit of sushi at *Harryhausen's* restaurant with his monster pals.

Big softy
Claws isn't actually as fierce as he looks. Nearly being touched by a child can reduce him to a big, blubbering blue mess.

Little horns

Officially the sharpest claws at Monsters, Inc.

Razor-sharp teeth

Short, spiky tail

Short legs

Did You Know?
Claws is close friends with fellow Scarers George and Nick "Lanky" Schmidt.

75

FUNGUS

GEEKY THREE-EYED Fungus has the terrifying task of being Randall's Assistant. His career may have blossomed with Randall's success, but the experience has made Fungus into a nervous monster. Secretly, he'd rather be inventing crafty contraptions than pandering to the loathsome lizard.

Always on call
Fungus is clever and hardworking – well, he has to be, working for a demanding monster like Randall!

Eyes wide open
Keeping Randall happy can be a terrifying business, and keeping his evil agenda secret is equally scary. Fungus has to keep all three eyes open, just in case something goes wrong.

Three-eyed glasses

Official Monsters, Inc. pass

Important Monsters, Inc. documents

Did You Know?
After Randall is banished to the human world, Fungus starts a new career making kids laugh for Monsters, Inc.

JERRY

AS THE FLOOR manager at Monsters, Inc., Jerry ensures everything runs flawlessly on the Scare Floor. Luckily, Jerry is an organised guy, so panicking monsters, shredded doors and contamination scares don't fluster him. He works hard to make sure that the maximum amount of screams is captured every day.

Scare challenge
Working on the Scare Floor is a challenge, but this doesn't frighten Jerry – in fact, he relishes his role as manager!

3-2-1-action!
Jerry counts down the seconds left for the monsters to get to work and start scaring.

Communications headset

"We may actually make our quota today!"

Multiskilled
Jerry has learned to deal with all the monstrous egos on the Scare Floor, and he is regarded as a key employee at Monsters, Inc. He even has a speaking part in the firm's TV commercial.

Did You Know?
Jerry has seven fingers on each hand – handy when he's doing countdowns for the monsters!

NEEDLEMAN AND SMITTY

NERDY NEEDLEMAN AND Smitty are the company janitors. This odd pair does lots of small but essential jobs, such as pushing carts of scream canisters and operating the door-shredding machine.

Monster fans
Needleman and Smitty are the monsters' biggest fans, and their hero is Sulley. Whenever he speaks to them, they erupt into a fit of nervous giggles.

Official Monsters, Inc. hard hat

A dirty job
Needleman and Smitty are a great team. They love their janitor jobs, even if the work is sometimes dirty – after all, they get to mingle with A-list celebrities like Sulley.

Big red nose

Official Monsters, Inc. hard hat

"Quiet! You're making him lose his focus."

Hard worker
Smitty is smitten with the stars of the Scare Floor, like Sulley – he thinks they are sooo cool. Smitty is a great monster to have around – he has a big heart and is always helpful.

Not so needle sharp
Needleman isn't the sharpest monster in the factory. However, he makes up for this with lots of enthusiasm, and he's a valued member of Monsters, Inc.

Four arms are better than two

Monsters, Inc. cleaning schedule

CHARLIE IS GEORGE Sanderson's Assistant on the Scare Floor. With two protruding eyes on stalks, he is great at spying trouble. Unfortunately, Charlie's tentacles are a little trigger-happy – he calls the Child Detection Agency at the slightest sign of a problem.

2319!
Charlie likes to be in the centre of the action at Monsters, Inc. He can often be heard shouting "2319" at the first sign of trouble. This is the code for an emergency, and makes the CDA come running.

Eyes on stalks always on the lookout for trouble

Did You Know?
Charlie manages to make it safely back from the Himalayas!

On the ball
Charlie is a very conscientious employee, but this has created problems for his clumsy friend George. Calling in the CDA resulted in George ending up on crutches with all of his fur shaved off!

Banished!
Charlie gets along well with George, and the two firm friends always have fun working in the factory. But George is a little tired of visits from the CDA, and before Charlie can make another call, George pushes him through a door to the Himalayas!

Three tentacle legs

DEAN HARDSCRABBLE

A LIVING LEGEND, this dean casts a long shadow over Monsters University. Dean Hardscrabble believes that monsters exist only to scare, and without that power, they are nobody. Having decided that Mike isn't scary, she considers him finished on the Scaring Program.

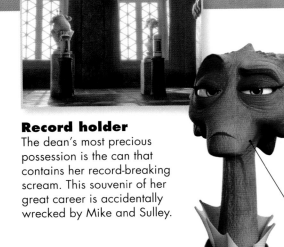

Record holder
The dean's most precious possession is the can that contains her record-breaking scream. This souvenir of her great career is accidentally wrecked by Mike and Sulley.

Menacing scowl

Games Master
When the expelled Mike and Sulley enter the Scare Games, Hardscrabble reluctantly agrees that if their team can win the games, they will be allowed on to the Scaring Programme. Of course, she believes they have no chance!

"Scariness is the true measure of a monster."

Always Right
Once this seasoned Scarer has decided that someone isn't scary, she never changes her mind. Being challenged by Mike and Sulley is a whole new experience for her, and one she treats with utter scorn.

Did You Know?
Hardscrabble founded the Scare Games when she was a student, and won four years in a row!

Scary, skittering legs

TOP SCARE STUDENT and president of the popular Roar Omega Roar fraternity, Johnny is the monster who seems to have everything. With brains as well as brawn, he rules the roost on campus and decides who is in the "in-crowd" and who gets left behind.

Super-scary horns

"RORs are the best Scarers on campus."

Team ROR

Johnny and his pals at ROR are all from rich, important families. They are cool, easygoing guys – while everything is going their way. But they turn nasty really fast if someone tries to outdo them.

Upturned collar

Roar Omega Roar crest

Big Bully

Mike is one of the main victims of Johnny's nasty side. The big college hero just can't stand little guys who don't know their place. He sneeringly calls Mike "Killer" and "beach ball".

Prankster

Sneaky Johnny uses a cruel sense of humour to put his enemies down. When Oozma Kappa impress in the Scare Games, he embarrasses them by tricking them into appearing in a cute photo with glitter confetti, flowers and stuffed animals!

SQUISHY

CHILDLIKE AND CHEERFUL, this nervous 19-year-old is the heart and soul of the Oozma Kappa gang. Squishy loves to make new members welcome, and if there is anything he can't personally provide, then his mum is happy to step in.

Sulley Fan
Squishy is thrilled to have some real scary monsters in the gang – the OKs are sure to do well in the Scare Games with Mike and Sulley on board.

"I've never stayed up this late in my life!"

Squishy snaps
Squishy rarely raises his voice, but he does get agitated when his mum is slow to drive off after their trip to Monsters, Inc. Ms Squibbles won't be rushed – she needs to check that all seat-belts have been fastened, and then wants to offer everyone a piece of gum!

Five eyes see more than one point of view

OK sweater knitted by mum

Games Hero
Squishy has a gift for fading into the background. It sure comes in handy in the "Avoid the Parent" Scare Games event, when he evades the librarian and takes the flag for his team!

Soft feet for creeping up on people

DON CARLTON

THIS MILD-MANNERED monster is the president of the OKs. Don learned a lot from his early years as a salesman – mainly that he wasn't wanted anymore! Now he has enrolled at MU as a mature student, seeking a new start.

Keep it down!

Deluded Don believed he was the master of the silent scare, until he found out just how noisy his suckers can be. His real talent lies in using them for hanging around in unexpected places!

Top Don

Don's leadership skills shine when the OKs make it to the Scare Games final. He steps out first in the head-to-head against ROR, and earns a high score in the simulator – putting OK in the lead!

Living the dream

Don has a permanently positive outlook on life: When he was let go by his sales company, he refused to throw a pity party and give up! Now he is learning about computers and getting reschooled in Scaring.

Big moustache

Business card

DON CARLTON
SALES

Did You Know?

One habit the ex-salesman can't quit is his fondness for handing out business cards. After his successes in the Scare Games, his cards now read "Scarer", rather than "Sales".

TERRI AND TERRY

THEY SAY THAT two heads are better than one, but this split personality isn't always so sure! One thing the Oozma Kappa brothers Terri and Terry Perry do share is a love of bickering – and a dream of becoming Scarers.

Party monsters
Terri and Terry have a gift for crazy dance routines, but can't always agree on when or where to perform them. The failed routine usually ends with an argument and public humiliation.

Disco ball drop
Terri and Terry plan a disco ball welcome party for new members Mike and Sulley. When it crashes straight to the floor, they confess they've never had a real party!

"You should wake up embarrassed!"

Double Trouble
Despite being physically inseparable, these brothers have very different personalities. "Terry with a 'y'" is older by several seconds, and sees himself as the wise, old cynic of the duo. "Terri with an 'i'" is the naïve youngster who often gets put in his place. But they can work together; their misdirection skills help the OKs confuse the librarian in the second Scare Games challenge.

Tea in a china cup

Extra arms are useful for magic tricks

ART

A creature of mystery, this new age philosophy student is a loyal member of Oozma Kappa. In a time of crisis, he can always be relied upon – to do something unexpected and bizarre!

Meditation Guru
Art is scared of working-out because he claims he is frightened of getting too big. He prefers meditation and yoga to exercise – as long as he can do it in his own unique way.

Dream Keeper
Art keeps a dream journal. It's a kooky habit he thinks everyone should practise – he even gives Mike and Sulley their own books to do it in.

Purple fuzz

Confession!
When nearly caught on the roof of Monsters, Inc., Art shocks his pals by confessing that he was once in prison!

Gapped teeth

Did You Know?
Art has a weird curiosity about everything – including touching the highly toxic glow urchins he was told to avoid in the first Scare Games event!

Mystery Monster
Prone to dropping baffling remarks about his past and hobbies, Art claims to have an extra toe (not that you can see it). He is also fond of sewer 14, which he says is his favourite of all the sewers on campus.

NEMO

A CUTE CLOWNFISH, Nemo lives with his devoted dad, Marlin, on a beautiful coral reef. Born with one small fin, Nemo is always eager to show his dad he can do anything other fish can do. One of his main tasks in life is to convince Marlin to lighten up and learn to trust others.

"I *can do* it, Dad."

Best buddies
An only fish, Nemo has always been very close to his dad, Marlin. The pair would be lost without each other – and Dory!

White stripes make Nemo harder for hungry predators to spot

In the tank
Nemo is scared of the fish in the aquarium at first. However, he soon learns that the Tank Gang are all lovable in their own weird ways.

Lucky fin

Caught!
On Nemo's first day of school, he was caught by a human diver and taken to live in an aquarium! Dory helped Marlin find him, and now the trio lives together in the coral reef.

Nemo uses his tail to push himself along

DORY

DORY MAKES FRIENDS everywhere she goes. The trouble is, she suffers from short-term memory loss, so she often forgets sea creatures as soon as she meets them. Dory loves helping others – she helps Marlin find Nemo when he goes missing. One day, Dory remembers she has her own problem – she has lost her family!

Big eyes to see in murky places

Down with the kids
Dory is a natural with kids, and turns Marlin into a legend of the seas when she tells the young turtle dudes all about his incredible adventures.

New family
To find her folks, Dory needs the help of Nemo and Marlin – two clownfish who have become her new family.

Yellow fin

"I think I lost somebody, but I can't remember."

Deep Dory
Dory is loaded with hidden talents. She can read human and she can also speak whale, which comes in handy when you're trapped inside one! When faced with the unknown, her motto is: "Just keep swimming".

Did You Know?
Dory is a regal blue tang. These fish have a powerful smell and can be poisonous, causing sickness and headaches if eaten.

MARLIN

MEET THE MOST overprotective parent in the sea! He is one of the biggest worriers, and he can't stop giving out safety tips. He is dedicated to bringing up his son Nemo, and also to being there for Dory. Deep down, he is incredibly brave – once he crossed the ocean to find his lost son.

Did You Know?
Clownfish live in the Indian and Pacific Oceans.

"I didn't come this far to be breakfast!"

A special layer of goo protects clownfish from anemone stings

Gloomy gills
When Marlin sees Dory taken safely into the Marine Life Institute, he worries it is a restaurant. Marlin always expects the worst!

Large eyes on the lookout for danger

Meeting Dory
It was a life-changing moment for Marlin when he first met Dory. She helped him to find Nemo and she taught him to never give up.

No clowning around
One of the problems with being a clownfish is people expect you to be funny. Marlin is not good at telling jokes and tends to see the downside of any situation. Luckily, Nemo and Dory always put a smile on his face.

CORAL

WITH A NEW home on the reef, a sea view and several hundred babies on the way, Coral seemed to have a sweet life in store for her – that is, until the dark day a big barracuda stopped by for dinner. In a terrible attack, Coral's dreams turned into a nightmare.

The name game
When Coral and Marlin visit the cosy hideaway of their big clutch of eggs, the only problem they can foresee in life is finding names for all of them.

Did You Know?
Clownfish produce anywhere from one hundred to a thousand eggs.

"There's over 400 eggs. Odds are, one of them is bound to like you."

Hopeful expression

Tail fin (personal rudder)

Hatching Nemo
Sadly, just one of Coral's eggs survives the terrible barracuda attack. Tiny Nemo keeps happy memories of Coral alive for Marlin.

Courageous Coral
Coral showed amazing courage in trying to protect her family, but she was gobbled up along with her eggs – well, all except one. The sole survivor was cherished by the heartbroken Marlin, and given a name that Coral liked: Nemo.

MR RAY

MR RAY IS MORE than just a teacher to his pupils at the Sandy Patch School. He is also an explorer of the seas. Full of enthusiasm, Mr Ray is an inspiring educator who loves to lead his class in song, using catchy songs to help them remember fascinating facts.

Pupil carrier
Transporting pupils on his wings, Mr Ray knows that his class will always be safe. At the reef, he lets them scatter and look around.

"Climb aboard, explorers!"

Class helper
Although she is an eager class assistant, Dory is not always very helpful to Mr Ray. She has trouble remembering facts and can wander off into trouble on class trips.

White dots help rays to hide in sand on the sea floor

Winglike fins for gliding through water

Ray of light
Mr Ray thinks of his charges not just as students, but as fellow undersea explorers. When teaching, he uses catchy rhymes to get across key facts: "Seaweed is cool, seaweed is fun, it makes its food from the rays of the sun!"

NEMO'S CLASS

NEMO'S CLASS IS made up of all kinds of reef fish. The children all seem to get along, but Mr Ray has two strict rules that the students must follow: learn and have fun! On his first day at school, Nemo makes three new friends.

Sheldon could sneeze at any moment

Dare scare
The three friends are dismayed when they lose their new friend Nemo on day one. A game of "touch the butt" (meaning the bottom of a boat) goes seriously wrong.

"Awwww! You guys made me ink!"

Sheldon
Sheldon is H_2O intolerant, so water makes him sneeze. That's an embarrassing problem for an ocean dweller!

Did You Know?
Unlike most species, the male seahorses, not the females, give birth to babies!

False "eyespot" fools predators

Tad
Tad the butterfly fish gets bored if he isn't the centre of attention. He often makes trouble in class and has to stay back and clean the eraser sponges.

Like any octopus, Pearl inks when excited or frightened

Pearl
This sweet little flapjack octopus has a small problem – when she gets excited, she squirts out ink. This might lead to a bit of teasing at school, but one day this skill could save Pearl's life from predators.

GILL

THE MOODY MASTERMIND of the Tank Gang, this Moorish idol fish believes that his kind were never meant to live in a box. From his lair in the plastic skull, Gill constantly dreams of freedom. He is never short of an escape plan – no matter how crazy and dangerous it is.

Thin body for slipping in among the crannies of coral reefs

Did You Know?
Moorish idol fish have colourful stripes, which help them to hide in the reef.

"All drains lead to the ocean, kid."

The mastermind
When Nemo arrives, Gill senses a promising new recruit and gives the clownfish a nickname: Sharkbait. Gill puts Nemo in peril with his daring plans, but when it really counts, the wily leader risks his life to set his friend free.

On the lookout
Gill may lay low most of the time, but his brilliant mind is always scheming. A deep thinker, he knows that all drains lead to the sea – and freedom.

BLOAT

BLOAT LOOKS LIKE any regular fish – until he gets mad, that is. When this short-tempered blowfish blows his cool, he puffs up into a spiky ball of rage. When Bloat was little, his big brother used to use him as a football, which just made him madder!

Fit to burst
Gill eventually leads the Tank Gang to the open ocean. When Bloat inflates excitedly, it is a tight squeeze in his plastic carry bag.

Brother bloat
Bloat puffs up with pride when he is given the big role in the Tank Gang ritual at Mount Wannahockaloogie.

Did You Know?
Blowfish are able to inflate because they have elastic skin and no ribs!

Fins used for flapping

Spines are poisonous

"You must pass through the Ring of Fire."

Ball of energy
Bloat's inflatable body is useful in an emergency, and he uses it to knock over the plastic volcano in one of Gill's escape attempts. The blowfish is an expert on extreme fish and master of ceremonies at the Ring of Fire initiation ceremony.

THIS HUMBUG FISH never feels lonely because she is convinced that her reflection is her identical twin sister! Deb finds Flo to be a loyal companion who is always there when she needs her. Her "sister" is never loud and is always in tune with her moods.

Jealous guys

Friends come by to visit Deb, but none of them seem to speak to Flo. Deb doesn't mind though – the tank guys are all just jealous of the special friendship she has with her twin!

Blue and white stripes

Deb's reflection (but don't tell her!)

Big eyes

"Don't listen to anything my sister says, she's nuts!"

In my face

There are a couple of drawbacks to having such an in-your-face friend. For a start, Flo sometimes blocks the view when Deb wants to look outside the tank. Deb also warns people to ignore whatever Flo says – because she's nuts!

JACQUES

BEYOND COMPARE IN the field of personal grooming, this classy cleaner shrimp maintains the highest standards of cleanliness. Jacques once belonged to the President of France, who gave him as a gift to the Australian Prime Minister, who then passed him on to the dentist.

"I am ashamed."

Helmet home
Jacques lives in this antique diver's helmet, which is not only a cosy home, but an escape from the scummy world outside and his disappointingly slimy friends.

Large eyes always on the lookout for specks of dirt

Jacques' helmet home

Magic touch
To Monsieur Jacques, cleaning isn't just a job – it's an art. When working on a new client, he really puts on a show and displays all the style and showmanship of a stage conjurer.

Squeaky-clean body

Long time no sea
Despite being named after the famous ocean explorer Jacques Cousteau, Jacques has never actually been in the real ocean. However, he considers this his good fortune – after all, the sea has no state-of-the-art filter system!

THE FISHTANK IN Dr Sherman's office is home to all sorts of fish. Nemo's terrified when he first arrives in the tank, but these guys quickly make him feel welcome and start helping to hatch a plan to get him back to the ocean.

Tank life

To outsiders, it's just a fish tank. But to Gill and the gang, it's home. With its bubbling electric volcano, Polynesian village and plastic gravel, it's a strange place to live!

Gurgle

Gurgle hates the idea of getting dirty. He's anxious around real-life reef fish like Nemo and is disgusted by a plan that involves making the tank filthy.

Gurgle's rainbow colours change depending on his mood

Did You Know?

If a starfish's arm is cut off, it will grow back again within a year!

Peach

This sharp-eyed starfish is the perfect lookout: She spends most of her time stuck to the side of the tank! She lets the others know when it's safe to start their escape plans.

Beady eyes always on the lookout

"Bubbles. Bubbles. My bubbles."

Bubbles

Suckers grab ahold of surfaces

Bubbles

As a tang fish, Bubbles could be related to Dory, which may explain his crazy ideas. He's always chasing bubbles, but he's never managed to catch one yet!

Bubbles is a yellow tang fish

NIGEL

HATCHED IN A nest on the roof of the dentist's office, Nigel has fancied himself as an expert on teeth ever since. He likes nothing better than to perch on the windowsill and talk with the Tank Gang about the tricky cases of the day, as long as he doesn't get shooed away by the dentist.

Did You Know?
Nigel has tried to get his pelican pals interested in dentistry, but they just want to sit atop the local bait shop and talk about how stupid seagulls are.

"Hop inside my mouth if you want to live."

Long, thin beak

Feel the pane
Although Dr P. Sherman is a nature lover, he does draw the line at Nigel treating his dentist's office as a social club. The friendly pelican loses more than a few feathers every week getting the window slammed in his face.

Pelican airways
Nigel's love of gossip comes in handy when he spots Marlin and Dory at the harbour boardwalk. He realises that these are fish on a mission and fearlessly flies to the rescue.

Nosy Nigel
Nigel is a friendly pelican with a very curious nature – he likes to stick his beak into everything. There's nothing Nigel doesn't know about the goings-on around Sydney Harbour.

Webbed feet – great for catching crumbs

BRUCE

G'DAY MATE! This terrifying eating machine is a reformed character – Bruce knows that if sharks want to shake off their nasty image, they first have to change themselves. He welcomes all marine life into his vegetarian community, sharing the notion that "fish are friends, not food".

Dangerous den
Bruce's gang think they have found the perfect hang-out – a wreck far from human eyes. But it's actually a sunken submarine, ringed with deadly unexploded mines!

Sharp teeth of a serious hunter

Party time
When Bruce invites fish to one of his parties, it's hard to say no! In fact, it's hard to say anything when you're petrified with fear.

Body built like a torpedo for speed

Food for thought
It's hard to relax around this grinning Great White. Bruce has the bad habit of calling smaller fish "morsels", and even the tiniest drop of blood in the water sends him into a feeding frenzy!

"Fish are friends, not food."

ANCHOR AND CHUM

ANCHOR AND CHUM are part of Bruce's vegetarian shark gang. Although they may look terrifying, they're both trying to give up eating fish. But reformed sharks can crack at any moment, so Anchor keeps a close eye on Chum to make sure he doesn't turn back into a savage seafood addict.

Did You Know?
Chum went to a posh predator boarding school. He worries that his hoity-toity friends will spot him fraternising with the local reef-raff.

Hammer-shaped head

Anchor
For a hammerhead, this guy's a softie, and likes nothing better than a group hug. Anchor doesn't always see eye-to-eye with his pals, which isn't surprising given the shape of his head.

Large back fin for swimming

Souvenir piercing

Huge, curved teeth

Sleek shark body

Chum
Check out Chum's cool face-piercing. This mean-looking shark got that souvenir from a run-in with a fisherman who'll think twice before angling for sharks again!

Clowning around
Anchor and Chum like nothing better than a good laugh and are excited to have a clownfish at one of their meetings. But Marlin can only fret about his lost son, and the gang conclude that he simply isn't very funny.

WHALE

Did You Know?
Whales can communicate with each other over miles of ocean using various forms of whale song.

LOOKS CAN BE deceiving under the sea, and this "little fella", as Dory calls him on first sight, turns out to be the biggest living creature in the ocean! The beautiful blue whale is grazing on some krill and swallows Marlin and Dory, too. They seem doomed to become his dinner…

Long, thin flippers

Whale talk
Not used to making dinner conversation with its own food, the whale is impressed with Dory's mastery of whale language. She can speak humpback and orca, as well as blue whale.

Pleated grooves expand during feeding

Big mouth swallows up to 40 million krill a day!

Kindly captor
The whale is gigantic, but gentle, too. It even gives Marlin and Dory a lift to their destination and a neat way back to the outside world – through its waterspout. The whale tells Dory when to let go, which is lucky, as letting go is not Marlin's strong suit!

Picking up passengers
Through their songs, whales can share news across whole oceans. So maybe this one knew all about Marlin's quest before it took him aboard…

CRUSH AND SQUIRT

CRUISING THE OCEANS in search of the perfect current, Crush and Squirt are the coolest turtles around. This pair of free spirits loves taking it easy and surfing around the Australian coast. They're always talking in surfer slang, calling everyone "dude" nonstop!

Crush

Despite their easygoing attitude, turtles are surprisingly tough and live for many years. Crush considers himself 150 years young, and still shows the little turtles who rules the gnarliest surf out there.

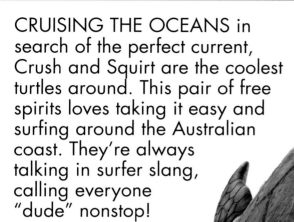

Streamlined shell to slide through the water

Strong beak for shredding snacks

Devoted dudes

Squirt loves to show his dad his latest stunts. When Crush is really impressed, they exchange a flippery high-five and an affectionate bump of the noggin.

Strong front flippers to ride the currents

Small back flippers

Squirt

Don't be fooled by this little dude's cute looks. Squirt is a tough kid who has already survived the ordeal of escaping clawing crabs and hungry seagulls right after being hatched.

DR SHERMAN

PHILIP SHERMAN uses his dental career to fund his real love – scuba diving. Philip tries to be considerate and only catches fish if he thinks they are struggling for life, which explains why he snaps up poor Nemo, with his weak fin.

"Crikey! All the animals have gone mad!"

Harbour views
P. Sherman often boasts of the views from his office. However, it seems the local wildlife prefer the view looking in on him!

Reef raider
Dr Sherman hits the reef every weekend in his boat, *The Aussie Flosser*. A rare find like Nemo is what he lives for.

Fish fanatic
Philip prefers his tank to teeth and even cancels dental appointments in order to clean out his fish tank. All his profits are spent on expensive plastic volcanoes and tiki idol heads to brighten up their lives. If only he knew that all his pets want is to escape!

Sherman would prefer to be wearing a wet suit

DARLA SHERMAN

DR SHERMAN'S NIECE, Darla, loves fish. She always checks out her uncle's amazing aquarium when she comes for her annual dental appointment on her birthday. She knows there's usually a gift in that tank for her and just hopes any new fish will survive a bit longer than the last one did...

"Yeah! Fishy, fishy, fishy!"

Bagging Nemo

It looks like the end for Nemo when he ends up bagged and at the mercy of Darla – as a very reluctant birthday present. It's as if she sees herself as a piranha, and all other fish as her prey.

Luxury brace set, received at special discount

Birthday bash

The Tank Gang live in fear of Darla's visits to the dentist's office. On every visit, she terrorises the poor fish, screaming at them and thumping on the tank to liven them up. She thinks her uncle has very sleepy fish. Maybe the silly gas gets to them, too?

Darla's favourite sweatshirt, a gift from her uncle

Great escape

The fish tormentor finally gets what she deserves when the Tank Gang fights back and helps Nemo to escape.

JENNY AND CHARLIE

DORY'S DOTING PARENTS would do anything for her, but what they do most is worry about her memory. They teach her games and songs to help her remember and stay safe… But their biggest fear comes true when she goes missing.

Reunited
Jenny and Charlie always knew that Dory was special. However, they are still amazed to hear about all the adventures she has had and all the friends she has made.

Shell paths
After Dory goes missing, her parents spend years making paths of shells. They hope that one day she will find one to follow all the way back home.

Did You Know?
Tangs really do like to live in pairs, just like Dory's mum and dad.

Body colour can change from light blue to dark blue or purple

Round and flat body

Flat, yellow tail

Charlie
A dedicated dad, Charlie teaches Dory that when problems seem impossible to solve, there is always another way, if you keep on trying. He loves playing with his daughter and calls her his little kelpcake.

Jenny
Always cheerful in front of Dory, Jenny secretly worries that her daughter will struggle on her own. She warns Dory that she must always stay away from the undertow – the strong current that could pull her away from them.

HANK

THIS GROUCHY OCTOPUS is actually a septopus – he lost one of his arms! All Hank wants is to be moved to a cosy aquarium in Cleveland, but Dory helps him see that life isn't only about helping yourself. At last, Hank has a reason to put his skills as a master of disguise into action.

Driving Dory
All those arms come in handy when Dory gives Hank his biggest challenge yet – driving a truck full of sea creatures!

Wanting out
When Hank first meets Dory in Quarantine, he sees her as his ticket to stay out of the ocean forever. He agrees to help her find her parents in exchange for her sick tag.

Did You Know?
The octopus is intelligent. It has a long-term and short-term memory, can use tools, and can solve problems.

Keen eyesight aids survival

All heart
A tough life has made Hank a seriously sulky guy. When Dory arrives, she brings friendship into his life and reminds him that someone with three hearts really ought to be a bit nicer.

Hank hangs on
Hank is not always in control. He has to rely on Dory to lead him to safety, away from the horrors of the touch pool.

Suction cups for sticking to things

Skin can change colour and texture

SEA LIONS

FLUKE AND RUDDER are two lazy sea lions who spend all day loafing around on the sunny rocks near the Marine Life Institute (MLI). The one activity that gets these two buddies excited is keeping their neighbour, Gerald, off their favourite basking space. Off! Off! Off!

Friendly favor
Gerald has one thing going for him – he's the owner of a bucket that he will lend out in exchange for a turn on the rock.

Rescued and released
As former residents, Fluke and Rudder know the MLI well. Now that they're fixed up, they are ready to do... as little as possible! If only Gerald would shove off and leave them to nap!

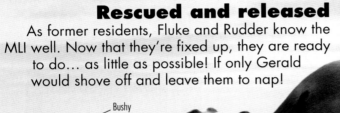

Bushy monobrow

Poor Gerald
When Marlin mentions that he and Nemo need water, they trick Gerald into giving up his pail by inviting him on their rock before kicking and shooing him off.

Short, thick fur

Long foreflipper

"We're trying to sleep!"

Helping hand
Sympathetic Fluke and Rudder are happy to help Marlin and Nemo get inside the MLI. They call on their friend Becky the loon bird to lend a helping wing.

Did You Know?
Sea lions can't breathe underwater – they have to hold their breath when diving.

BECKY

SHE MAY NOT look that bright, but this likable loon bird understands instructions as long as you get in sync with her. Still, Marlin is not sure he can trust Becky to give him and Nemo a lift, especially with all the crazy noises she has to make!

Getting pecky
Marlin is not thrilled when he finds out Becky will be giving him a lift. She keeps pecking him!

Feathered friend
Becky is a friend to Fluke and Rudder. She helps them out if they ask her very politely.

"Ooo-roooo!"

Heavy wings make lift-off tricky

Tuning in
The only way to get through to Becky is to imprint yourself on her by making loon noises and staring her in the eye. After that, she'll never forget you.

Frequent flyer
A regular visitor to the Marine Life Institute, Becky flies in for delicious snacks of popcorn. She can usually rely on tourists to drop a cup or two throughout the day.

Did You Know?
Loon birds are famous for their calls. In winter, they make a long, sad, but beautiful wail.

Webbed feet for swimming

DESTINY

ONE OF THE stars of the MLI, Destiny is a whale shark who was rescued after her poor eyesight meant she became a nervous swimmer. She and Dory go way back. The two friends used to talk through the pipes in their pools. Dory loved hearing Destiny's funny stories again and again.

"We were pipe pals!"
With Dory's bad memory and Destiny's poor eyesight, it takes a while for these two old friends to recognise each other.

Very wide mouth

Thick, protective skin

Unique personal spot pattern

A new destiny
A little support from her friends is all Destiny needs to return to the wild. She is worried about bumping into things, but her good friends offer to be her eyes as she makes her leap to freedom.

Bailey's buddy
Destiny is never short of someone to talk to with Bailey in the pool next door. They know each other well enough to put up with a little playful banter.

Did You Know?
The whale shark's only known predator is the human.

Pool home
Destiny has a state-of-the-art pool to swim in, but with her poor eyesight, she has trouble avoiding crashing into the walls.

BAILEY

BAILEY IS A rescued beluga whale, now attracting crowds to the MLI. He suffered a blow to the head in the wild, which he believes gave him a swollen head and affected his ability to echolocate. He never stops worrying about his injury. But, in fact, all belugas look like him!

"My head hurts!"

Bulbous head

White skin for camouflage in ice

Flippers have rounded edges

Echo power
It takes a crisis to get Bailey's confidence up. When Dory needs his help, he finds the courage to try out his echolocation. It's working just fine!

Bouncing back
This moody mammal thinks his echolocation skills are broken, but Destiny isn't so sure. She believes in Bailey and knows he's just about as perfect as a beluga can be. All he really needs is a bit of confidence!

Practically family
Destiny and Bailey know each other well. They have spent so long together, they act like brother and sister.

FINDING DORY

MR INCREDIBLE

BOB PARR, a.k.a. Mr Incredible, was once the greatest Super of them all. But then he saved someone who didn't want to be saved, got sued, and was driven into hiding with the rest of his Super family. A normal life beckoned, but Bob is just too big a hero to fit into the everyday world.

Heroic dad
When his wife is called away on a new mission, Bob becomes a stay-at-home dad. He wishes he could be a Super again, too!

Gloved hand

The Incredibles logo

Stylish new suit, courtesy of Edna Mode

Glory days
Keeping the city safe was all in a day's work for Mr Incredible back in his Super glory days. For a while, it seemed he had the world at his feet.

Did You Know?
As well as being super-strong, Mr Incredible is fast and agile. His one weakness is a slightly bad back.

Back in action
Mr Incredible is lured out of retirement by a mysterious message offering him the chance to go on a top-secret mission. He is soon on a plane bound for Nomanisan Island and taking on the sinister villain Syndrome. But Bob eventually realises that his family is really his biggest adventure.

"Just like old times"

ELASTIGIRL

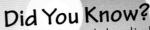

Did You Know?

Helen can stretch her limbs up to 30 metres (98 feet). She can also squeeze through the tiniest cracks.

HELEN PARR, a.k.a. Elastigirl, was one of the top Supers on the planet, with the power to stretch her body into any shape imaginable. When Elastigirl met Mr Incredible, it was love at first sight, and together they make an incredible team.

Cool costume

Helen gets a new suit for her public return to crime-fighting. It features a tiny camera to record her heroic actions.

Doting wife

When she notices that her husband's old costume has been repaired, Helen sets off on a mission to find out why and discovers he is in peril. She packs her new Super suit and flies to Nomanisan Island. Boldly facing any danger, Helen proves that she is still Super.

Super mum

When the Supers first went into hiding, Helen was happy to trade the challenges of vanquishing evil for the joys of raising kids. But when she gets a taste of her old Super life, she realises she must return to crime-fighting.

Helen's suit is virtually indestructible

Chosen Super

Winston and Evelyn invite Elastigirl to help them with their scheme to make Supers legal again. They have already persuaded some other Supers to join them in their effort to regain public support.

Helen is as Super as she ever was!

"Leave the saving of the world to the men? I don't think so!"

VIOLET PARR

A SMART TEENAGER, Violet Parr yearns for a normal life. She has learned to hide her feelings behind a sarcastic attitude, and her face behind her long dark hair. It takes a family crisis to make Violet realise just how much she has to offer.

Violet no longer hides behind her hair

Crush crisis
Despite gaining confidence when she becomes a Super, things still don't go Violet's way with her crush Tony Rydinger. Tony has his mind wiped and stands Violet up – all thanks to her dad!

Shrinking Violet
Violet used to like hiding away in the background of family life. She listened to music and read beauty magazines in her quest to fit in at school and be like everyone else.

"Normal? What does anyone in this family know about being normal?"

Visible progress
Now you see her – now you don't! Violet has a tricky time exploiting her powers until brilliant fashion designer Edna Mode creates a special Super suit for her. As Vi's confidence grows, so does her power. She even brushes back her hair and shows the world how incredible she really is.

Feel the force
When danger strikes the family, Violet's true power emerges. In addition to her invisibility, she finds she can create unbreakable spherical force fields.

Practical, stylish thigh-high boots

DASH PARR

DASH IS HIS NAME and speed is his game! It's hard for Dashiell Parr to be the fastest thing on Earth *and* keep his cool power a secret – especially as he is only 10 years old! Dash has to console himself by playing faster-than-light pranks at school – such as sticking pins on his teacher's chair.

Making a splash
While fleeing Syndrome's minions on Nomanisan Island, Dash makes a cool discovery – he is so fast that he can run right across the water's surface!

Windswept hair

Teacher's pest
Being the son of heroes doesn't make Dash super well-behaved or want to do his maths homework. He often gets into trouble at school, and a trip back from the Principal's office with mum is not an unusual event.

Determined expression

Fast learner
When the family is called into action, Dash finds that he has a lot to learn. First, all bad guys aren't like the ones on TV shows – they're much scarier – and second, his powers are way cooler than he realised.

Little legs can run super-fast

"I promise I'll slow up. I'll only be the best by a tiny bit."

JACK-JACK PARR

THE NEWEST MEMBER of the Incredible family, Jack-Jack Parr is seriously cute and his parent's pride and joy. As far as his family knows, Jack-Jack has no super powers – unless it's throwing food, jabbering and being super cute! But maybe he's just a slow developer…

Talented tot
Jack-Jack has even more powers than his family combined! Over time, he reveals he can create many copies of himself, grow to become a giant baby and even change his appearance to look like another person.

Jack-Jack's hair never needs gel

Monster mode
Turning into a monster is just one of the surprise talents Jack-Jack has been hiding from his parents. He can also defy gravity, pass through walls and shoot energy beams from his eyes!

Even a baby needs to protect his secret identity!

Baby Super
When Syndrome kidnaps Jack-Jack, the tiny tot reveals his awesome transforming powers as a shape-shifter. He turns into living fire, becomes as heavy as lead and then transforms into a mad mini-fiend. In short, he's too hot to handle.

Did You Know?
Jack-Jack can also turn himself into a gooey form, so that things stick to him!

Baby Super suit

FROZONE

LUCIUS BEST, A.K.A. Frozone, was the coolest Super around. Thanks to his wit and style, and an amazing arsenal of freezing powers, Frozone was one cool customer. Although he seems to have adjusted to civilian life better than his pal Bob, he has kept his Super suit and gadgets.

Did You Know?

The downside of being Frozone is having people make jokes about your power all the time. He has heard Bob's "ice of you to drop by" many times!

"You tell me where my suit is, woman! We're talking about the greater good!"

Family friend

Lucius is best pals with Mr Incredible, and the whole Parr family adores him. Every Wednesday, Bob and Lucius get together. Their wives think they go bowling – but really they hang out listening to the police radio and reliving their glory days.

Snow motion

Frozone has plenty of cool tricks for getting out of trouble. Ice-skis help him ski-jump to safety.

Awesome ally

Frozone is always there to get the Incredibles out of hot water. He freezes up the street when the Omnidroid attacks Municiberg, and he uses his icy powers to help the family stop the Underminer from destroying City Hall.

SYNDROME

AFTER MR INCREDIBLE rejects him as a sidekick, Buddy Pine reinvents himself as the villain Syndrome. An evil genius bent on revenge, Syndrome turns Nomanisan Island into his high-tech hideaway and terminates every Super he can get his gloves on.

Incrediboy
To start with, Buddy Pine called himself Incrediboy, but he was merely an incredible nuisance. He distracted Mr Incredible on the disastrous mission that ended with the great hero being sued.

Monologuing maniac
When Syndrome finally captures Mr Incredible, it is the moment he has spent 15 years waiting for. However, like all crazy villains, Syndrome is easily tempted into blurting out his evil plans – big mistake.

"I'll be a bigger hero than you ever were."

Cape proves to be a fatal mistake for Syndrome

Hoax hero
Syndrome's master plan is to menace Municiberg with his evil Omnidroid, then pretend to defeat it and be hailed as a great new hero. Fortunately, just as he did all those years ago, Mr Incredible is there to upset Buddy's plans.

Jet boots

MIRAGE

SYNDROME'S accomplice, the alluring and mysterious Mirage, has all the charm and people skills that he lacks. Highly skilled with technology and a master of surveillance, she tracks down the Supers that her boss has targeted, then lures them into action – for the last time.

Immaculate platinum-blonde hair

Did You Know?
Mirage is so good at spying undercover that, according to the government, she doesn't even officially exist!

"Next time you gamble, bet your own life!"

Secret identity
When Mr Incredible arrives at Nomanisan Island, Mirage knows how to act as the perfect hostess. She flatters him, pampers his ego and prepares him for his mission, without once giving away any of her master's real plan.

Slinky satin dress

Changing sides
Mirage confesses that she has a weakness for power. She is loyal to Syndrome until she comes to respect a different kind of strength – the kind that holds the Incredible family together. Mirage knows it's time to change teams.

Life saver
Being held captive, Mr Incredible has a chance to finish Mirage but he doesn't take it. She is grateful – and impressed by his humanity.

Heels for added height

EDNA MODE

Did You Know?
Edna demands to be the exclusive Super-suit designer for the Incredibles from now until the end of time!

WORLD-FAMOUS fashion designer Edna "E" Mode is vain, opinionated and outspoken. She is also brilliant. Her exclusive collections are modelled on catwalks all over the world, but E longs for the days when she created costumes for Supers – and made them look simply fabulous, darling!

Safety first
Edna is obsessed with security. To enter her studio, visitors must pass electric fences, video cameras, and handprint, eyeprint and voiceprint checks!

Super-slick hair

New challenge
This fast-talking fashion guru can talk anyone into anything. When Bob drops by for a small costume repair, Edna is inspired to reoutfit the whole family – whether they like it or not.

"I never look back, darling. It distracts from the now."

Power dressing
Edna is thrilled to design new suits for Bob and his family. Her new range of costumes combine the strength of mega-mesh with new qualities that imitate the powers of the wearer. Edna does insist on sticking to one rule though – no capes!

Edna designs all of her own stylish outfits

Super design
Edna creates a new, improved suit for Jack-Jack, which has sensors to detect the power he will use next. The sensors alert the family via a monitor.

GILBERT HUPH

THE BOSS OF Insuricare, Gilbert Huph only cares about making a profit, and if that means not paying little old ladies what they're owed, that's fine by Huph. A small-minded man with a pea-sized heart, he is a very big bully in a very little body. Unfortunately, he is also Bob Parr's boss.

Not happy!
Huph has a serious problem with Bob, who actually wants to help people. He summons Bob to his office, determined to put a stop to his caring attitude towards customers.

Final straw
Bob loses his cool when halfway through Huph's lecture, Bob sees a man being mugged outside and is unable to help him because Huph threatens to fire him.

> "Tell me how you're keeping Insuricare in the black!"

Huph permanently has the hump

Did You Know?
Insuricare has a wide range of customers. Bob usually advises them on how to get around their big bad bureaucracy!

Neatness nut
Gilbert is fixated on order. He likes his pencils neat and tidy and expects his life to be the same. He thinks a company is like an enormous clock, in which all the little cogs have to do their job – make money.

Hospital case
Huph finally pushes Bob too far and gets pushed right back – through several office walls. Gilbert has plenty of time to worry about his own health insurance while lying in a hospital bed.

BOMB VOYAGE

AN EXPERT WITH explosives, Bomb Voyage is a stylish super-criminal. He wears the make-up of a French mime artist and conducts all of his in-fight banter in French. Don't be disarmed, however, by his quirky appearance – this eccentric evil-doer is a ruthless fiend, equipped with an ammo belt loaded with deadly bombs.

Familiar foe
Bomb Voyage is an old adversary of Mr Incredible, and neither are at all surprised to bump into each other during the raid at the Municiberg bank.

"Your outfit is totally ridiculous!"

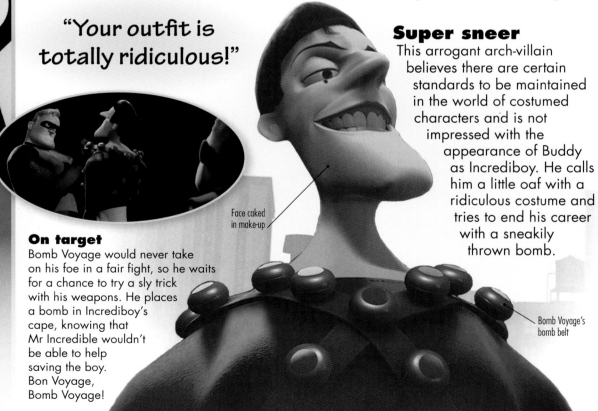

On target
Bomb Voyage would never take on his foe in a fair fight, so he waits for a chance to try a sly trick with his weapons. He places a bomb in Incrediboy's cape, knowing that Mr Incredible wouldn't be able to help saving the boy. Bon Voyage, Bomb Voyage!

Face caked in make-up

Super sneer
This arrogant arch-villain believes there are certain standards to be maintained in the world of costumed characters and is not impressed with the appearance of Buddy as Incrediboy. He calls him a little oaf with a ridiculous costume and tries to end his career with a sneakily thrown bomb.

Bomb Voyage's bomb belt

THE UNDERMINER

JUST WHEN THE Incredibles think they have saved Municiberg from the forces of evil, up pops another threat to the city. This molelike monster has come to declare war on peace and happiness – but he has chosen the wrong place to start his career. The Incredibles are there, ready to overpower the Underminer.

To the rescue again
The Parr family shouldn't have put their civilian clothes back on so fast. There's a new bad guy in town and he's out to cause trouble!

"Behold, the Underminer! I'm always beneath you, but nothing is beneath me!"

Tunnel visionary
This diabolical digger wears a miner's helmet with a lamp, so he can see in the dark tunnels he has created beneath the city. No obstacle can block his way, as he travels everywhere in an earth-shaking drilling machine.

Bright light for seeing in dark tunnels

Hard hat

Bank heist
The Underminer doesn't count on facing the Incredibles and Frozone when he robs Municiberg's bank vaults. But the tunnelling terror still manages to escape!

WINSTON DEAVOR

THIS RICH, SUAVE and brilliant businessman is the Supers' biggest fan. He wants to use his super wealth and power to legalise Supers again and to bring them out of the shadows so that they can make the world a safer place for all.

Super scheme
Winston and Evelyn pick Elastigirl as the face of their campaign. They put a tiny camera in Elastigirl's Super suit that records her saving the day. They plan to show the footage to the public to create positive publicity for Supers.

Charming smile

Ridiculously expensive suit

Incredible wealth
Winston owns DevTech, a telecommunications company, with Evelyn. He has fancy cars, a private jet, a high-tech yacht and so many mansions that he lets the Incredibles stay in one for free – for as long as they like!

Supers are good!
Along with his sister, Evelyn, Winston launches a Supers image rehabilitation campaign to regain the public's support of the heroes. He hopes to persuade the government to make Supers legal again. Winston just needs to find the perfect hero to front the campaign.

Huge fan
Winston has always been a superfan of Supers. He knows many of their theme songs by heart.

EVELYN DEAVOR

GENIUS INVENTOR EVELYN creates all the innovative products for DevTech, the hugely successful tech company she owns with her brother, Winston. Evelyn loves her brother, but she doesn't always agree with him… he just has no idea quite how much!

Messy crop

Did You Know?
Evelyn has been inventing since she was a young child. She knows everything there is to know about technology.

"Thanks. Designed 'em myself."

A close bond
Evelyn is so friendly that Elastigirl easily opens up to her. She soon gains the Super's trust – but can Evelyn be trusted?

Casual clothes

Talented team
Kindhearted and helpful, Evelyn seems eager to support Winston in his plan to get the Supers legalised. While Winston uses his salesman skills to sell the idea that Supers are good, Evelyn brings her incredible intelligence and amazing technical skills to the planning.

Extraordinary inventions
Evelyn designs a hidden camera for Elastigirl's Super suit and her high-tech bike. The Elasticycle breaks up into two bikes so that Elastigirl can stretch between them.

THE SCREENSLAVER

THIS MYSTERIOUS Screenslaver highjacks techology to manipulate people from a distance. The high-tech supervillain can hack any screen to broadcast patterns that hypnotise viewers in an instant. But who is hiding behind the mask?

Glowing goggles

Hyp–no way!
Elastigirl tracks the Screenslaver to his lair. The sinister supervillain hides in the shadows, ready to attack with his terrifying array of hypnotising screens, lights, and weapons. But Elastigirl still overpowers him!

Did You Know?
The Screenslaver sets up a hypno-clock device to blow up his flat – and all the evidence! – while he flees.

Dingy den
The Screenslaver's apartment is full of research notes and plans of attack.

The Screenslaver dresses head-to-toe in black

Message
The manipulative menace hijacks screens to rant about humanity. He thinks people are lazy and that Supers are harmful to society because normal people rely on them to save the day – rather than doing anything themselves.

"Screenslaver interrupts this programme for an important announcement."

WANNABE SUPERS

ELASTIGIRL'S HEROIC ACTIONS inspire others with awesome abilities to want to become Supers, too. A group of wannabe Supers team up as part of the Deavors' campaign to paint Supers in a more favourable light. But things don't go to plan when the wannabes are hypnotised and ordered to kidnap the Parr children.

Cool blue hair

Did You Know?
Voyd hero-worships Elastigirl but ends up fighting her idol while under hypnosis.

Voyd
Shy Voyd is a big fan of Elastigirl. Voyd can create portals that can move people and objects from one place to another.

Lightning-bolt design

He-lectrix
This stylish Super manipulates electricity. He shoots lightning bolts from his fingertips.

Reflux
Elderly, kind Reflux has a serious case of heartburn. He can spew hot lava from his mouth!

Unsettled tummy

"K" for Krushauer

Krushauer
This hulking Super can not only crush things with his hands, but with his mind, too.

Brick
Muscular Brick has incredible strength. She can expand her body so that she becomes as big and strong as a brick wall.

Even Brick's belt features a brick

Handmade owl-like wings

Screech
This Super can fly, thanks to the wings that he constructed himself. His owl-like screech is so powerful it can break glass.

PISTON CUP LEGEND Lightning McQueen is the greatest race car of his generation. Focused and fast, he has an awesome record of results. Although he's a celebrity, his pals in Radiator Springs ensure his wheels remain firmly on the ground.

Big entrance
Lightning causes mayhem when he accidentally crashes through the sleepy town of Radiator Springs. But all the residents grow to love him – eventually!

Tough competition
Lightning McQueen is surprised by the success of rookie racer Jackson Storm. When the brash newbie starts to get results, McQueen realises he has a serious rival.

"Speed. I am speed."

Star car
Lightning finds life in the fast lane a real gas – lapping up attention from fans and being treated like a star car. But life at the top can be lonely, and Lightning never forgets that his pals are more important than his career.

Did You Know?
Hotshot race car Lightning has won the Hudson Hornet Memorial Cup once and the Piston Cup an amazing seven times!

Lightning always races in red

MATER

RUSTY TOW TRUCK Mater runs Radiator Springs' salvage centre. He keeps the residents entertained with his wicked sense of humour and huge sense of fun. Loyal Mater is always willing to help his friends and pull them through any crisis.

Disguises and surprises
Mater has a host of disguises and weapons fitted by Agent Holley Shiftwell in a mission to catch the Lemons. They include a rocket-powered jet and computer-generated disguises!

"I'm the world's best backwards driver!"

Firm friends
Mater's a rusty tow truck and Lightning's a celebrity, but they are still best buddies. Mater usually stays at home when Lightning goes off to race – until the WGP, when Mater becomes part of Team Lightning McQueen!

New adventure
Before meeting Lightning, Mater never left Radiator Springs. But a case of mistaken identity at the World Grand Prix (WGP) sees Mater thrust into a secret mission with the British Intelligence. Mater soon proves he is one brave tow truck.

The fastest tow-rope in Carburetor County!

Buck teeth

DOC HUDSON

DOC HUDSON IS ONE of the most respected residents of Radiator Springs. As the town's motor-medic, he gives the citizens thorough checkups at his medical clinic. He is also the town judge. Sadly, Doc is no longer with us, but his spirit lives on in Radiator Springs.

Doc's orders
Doc challenges Lightning to a race at Willy's Butte to teach the arrogant youngster a thing or two. Sure enough, the wise Doc wins and Lightning ends up in a bed of cacti!

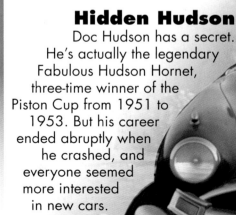

Back on track
Doc goes back to the racetrack to support Lightning as his crew chief. With a Fabulous Hudson Hornet paint job from Ramone, the racing legend wins a round of applause from the crowd.

"Was that floating like a Cadillac, or was that stinging like a beemer?"

Hidden Hudson
Doc Hudson has a secret. He's actually the legendary Fabulous Hudson Hornet, three-time winner of the Piston Cup from 1951 to 1953. But his career ended abruptly when he crashed, and everyone seemed more interested in new cars.

Shiny chrome

SALLY

BRILLIANT AND BEAUTIFUL, sleek Sally runs the *Cozy Cone* Motel in Radiator Springs. She used to live life in the fast lane as a lawyer until she discovered Radiator Springs and fell in love with the town and its residents. The plucky Porsche is determined to do all she can to put her beloved town back on the map.

Did You Know?
Sally sports a small, pinstripe tattoo on her rear. When Lightning notices it, Sally is very embarrassed!

Road to romance
When Sally meets Lightning, she is not impressed by his smart one-liners or the revving of his engine. Later, on a long drive through Carburetor County, Sally discovers a kinder, more open-hearted Lightning.

Legal whizz
Sally still uses her legal training as the town's attorney. She has a strong sense of justice and is very confident in court.

"Do you want to stay at the *Cozy Cone* or what?"

Grand plans
Sally is a car with big dreams and grand schemes. She plans to reopen the legendary *Wheel Well* Hotel on Route 66, which will really help get the forgotten town back on the map.

Lightweight alloy wheels

GUIDO

COMPACT ITALIAN forklift Guido is the fastest tyre changer in town, and probably the world! He works with his best pal Luigi at *Casa Della Tyres*. The tiny forklift has a big dream – to change the tyres on a real race car, preferably a Ferrari!

Proud pitty
At the Piston Cup, Guido does Radiator Springs (and Italy) proud. During the tie-breaker race, he performs a pit stop on Lightning so quick that his movements are a blur.

Luigi is happiest when he's changing tyres

"Pit stop!"

True colours
At Willy's Butte, Guido shows his support for Lightning – by waving a Ferrari flag!

Fastest forklift around

Dream come true
The fanatical forklift's ultimate dream to be a pitty is realised twice – first at the Piston Cup and again at the WGP. At both races, nimble Guido shrugs off the doubts of the other pit crews and really shows them how it's done!

LUIGI

LUIGI IS THE owner of *Casa Della Tyres*. A 1959 Fiat 500, he brings Italian flair, passion and some fast talking to the sleepy town of Radiator Springs. Whether you need advice on a stylish set of tyres or just a friend to talk to, lovable Luigi will never let you down.

Ferrari fan
Luigi is crazy about racing, especially Ferraris. Meeting Lightning is a big thrill for him – until he learns that Lightning doesn't know any Ferraris.

Home sweet home
Luigi and Guido get to visit Uncle Topolino, their favourite uncle in Porta Corsa, Italy, when they travel there as part of the WGP. Years ago, they worked in his tyre shop, *Topolino's*, where he gave them the inspiration to open their own tyre shop.

Retractable, fabric sunroof

Bella Italia
Luigi is big-hearted and excitable. His energy and enthusiasm rub off on everyone around him, and his lively personality always sends customers on their way with an extra spring in their suspension.

"Luigi follow only the Ferraris."

Fiat hood ornament

RAMONE

RAMONE IS A 1959 Chevrolet and the coolest car in Radiator Springs. He runs his *House of Body Art*, Radiator Springs' custom paint shop, and makes sure he gives himself a new coat of paint several times a week. Ramone is often seen out cruising with his wife, Flo.

Cool customer
Before Lightning sets off to show the world what he's made of at the WGP, he stops off at Ramone's to get a brand new paint job. Ramone works his magic, and Lightning looks brand new!

Arty car
Ramone is an artist with an airbrush and a magician with paint and metal. Whether you want a flame job, ghost flames or even some old-school pinstripes "Von Dutch" style, Ramone will paint you right up.

True romance
Ramone and Flo's relationship is as strong as the day they first met, and they have become Radiator Springs' premier couple!

Flashy flame paint job

Hydraulics allow Ramone to ride high or low

"Oh yeah, baby!"

FLO

FLO IS A CLASSIC show car from the 1950s. Sassy and sleek, she has been running *Flo's V8 Café* for years. Everyone knows the town would fall apart without Flo – there would be no one to sell gasoline and oil, or dish out sage advice.

Heart and soul
Cars are guaranteed a warm welcome at *Flo's V8 Café*. The town's residents gather there every day to sip oil and catch up on local gossip.

Come on in
Friendly Flo is always on the lookout for new customers to dazzle with her unique brand of Carburetor County hospitality.

"I have gas! Lots of gas!"

Flo's show
As a show car, Flo used to travel across the country, modelling her beautiful curves and swooping fins. When she passed through Radiator Springs, she fell in love with Ramone and never left the little town.

Flo is always spotless

Super-sleek curves

Knock-out smile

SHERIFF

STRAIGHT-TALKING, hardworking and honest, Sheriff is driven by a strong sense of duty – protecting the good citizens of Radiator Springs. He takes the job very seriously: Any troublemakers will be taken straight to Traffic Court, and Sheriff may even siphon off their gas so they can't escape!

Nap time
Radiator Springs is a sleepy town where lawbreaking is rare. This means that Sheriff can often be found taking a nap at his favourite spot behind the billboard.

Take a break
Sheriff loves to drop in at *Flo's V8 Café* for a quart of oil and to tell stories about his days on the old Highway 66.

"I haven't gone this fast in years. I'm gonna blow a gasket or somethin'."

Worn-out cop
Sheriff is not in tip-top condition. Pursuing Lightning McQueen at high speeds leaves the law enforcer exhausted; in fact, he backfires so many times, Lightning thinks he's being shot at! Perhaps Sheriff has just enjoyed too much oil at *Flo's V8 Café*.

Gotcha!
When Lightning McQueen breaks the speed limit, Sheriff is already waiting on the edge of town to try and catch him!

Siren ensures the Sheriff is heard before he is seen

Tendency to backfire at high speeds

SHERIFF

RED

RED IS RADIATOR SPRINGS' only fire truck and the town's most sensitive resident. He is a quiet and gentle soul, but he's devoted to his community. In an emergency, Red is always the first to spring into action!

Friend in need
When Sally sees how dirty Lightning has become after working on the road, she asks Red to help out...

Water truck
Red always puts his hose to good use. There aren't many fires in Radiator Springs, so Red spends his time watering all the town's plants and flowers. He wants to make sure that Radiator Springs is always looking its blooming best!

Spray hello
Lightning is surprised when Red suddenly blasts him with cold water – but he's a lot cleaner afterward!

Extra hosepipe lengths for hard-to-reach flowers

Fire hose

Official fire department emblem

FILLMORE

AGING HIPPIE Fillmore owns *Fillmore's Taste-In,* where he brews his own organic fuel. His fuel comes in a variety of flavours, including Glubble and Gastro Blastro. The only vehicle in town with tie-dye mud flaps and an interest in automotive yoga, Fillmore often spars with Sarge.

Unlikely pals
Sarge thinks Fillmore is a hippie freak because of his peace-loving views. Although these two always bicker, they can't live without each other.

Tasty brew
Lightning drops by *Fillmore's Taste-In* to take the fuel taste test before he leaves for the Piston Cup rematch. He thinks it's so good, he orders a case to take with him.

Wonder fuel
Fillmore believes in peace, love and organic fuel! When he learns that the WGP will be run exclusively on the alternative fuel Allinol, Fillmore closes up shop and signs on as the fuel expert for Team Lightning.

Environmental stickers

Laid-back expression

Paintings are Fillmore's own designs

CARBURETOR
51237
COUNTY

SARGE

EX-ARMY JEEP Sarge brings military discipline to Radiator Springs. He runs *Sarge's Surplus Hut*, which is polished to a shiny sheen and fronted by a super-neat lawn. Sarge has traditional views and disagrees with hippie cars like Fillmore. However, his bark is worse than his bite, and he can always be relied on to help his pals.

Opposites attract

Sarge lives next door to Fillmore. His tidy hut and garden is the complete opposite to Fillmore's free-flowin' backyard.

Attention!

Sarge brings a sense of duty and military discipline to Team Lightning McQueen at the WGP – when he's not bickering with Fillmore, that is.

"Oh, take a carwash, hippie."

Military mind

Being from a military background, Sarge follows a highly disciplined routine. Each morning, the patriotic soldier raises the Stars and Stripes and salutes it with his antenna. Fillmore's less happy about being woken up by the trumpets of "Reveille"!

Did You Know?

Sarge served in the military, where he received the Grille Badge of True Mettle for his bravery.

LIZZIE

LIZZIE IS Radiator Springs' most senior citizen. Nevertheless, she's got more gumption than cars half her age. With her mischievous sense of humour, occasional outspoken comments and unreliable memory, many townsfolk think she's slightly bonkers!

Legend
Lizzie was married to Stanley, who founded Radiator Springs in 1909. He is immortalised as a statue outside the fire station, and Lizzie visits it every day, remembering the good times they had together.

Lizzie's Wares
Lizzie owns a curio shop, and she can often be found taking a well-earned nap outside. The shop sells everything from Route 66 memorabilia to souvenir snow globes.

"You keep talking to yourself, people will think you're crazy!"

Did You Know?
Lizzie first drove into Radiator Springs in 1927. Although Stanley had to ask Lizzie out a few times before she actually said yes, the pair soon became inseparable.

Plain speaker
Lizzie believes in always telling it like it is, no matter what others may think (even if she can't remember exactly what "it" is!) Her straight-talking comments often surprise the younger inhabitants of Radiator Springs.

Squeaky parts need plenty of oil

THE FIELDS AROUND Radiator Springs are full of tractors, happily grazing, munching and chewing. These creatures aren't clever – they eat and sleep and then eat and sleep a bit more. The tractors are supervised by Frank – a combine harvester and 10 tonnes of angry agricultural machinery.

Tractor tipping

Tractors are dozy, docile and dopey. They are the perfect targets for Mater's favourite pastime – tractor tipping. One honk from the cheeky tow truck and the tractors are so startled, they tip over backwards!

Mud splotches

Arghhhhh!

Mater takes Lightning for some tractor tipping late one night, but fun turns to fear when Frank appears on the scene. As he comes after Mater and Lightning, they do what any car would do – flee!

Fierce Frank

Frank the Combine doesn't take kindly to anyone messing with his tractors. If anyone upsets him or his tractors, ferocious Frank will chase after them. When his rotating blades are bearing down on you, it's probably time to make a run for it.

Beware of Frank's rotating blades!

THE KING

STRIP "THE KING" Weathers is racing royalty. Not only has he won seven Piston Cups, but he has also won over virtually everyone he's met. This track legend is the perfect professional – a true gent and good sport on and off the track. He's just a regular guy who regularly wins everything!

Pushing in

In The King's final race of his final season, he crashes yards from the finish line, after being slammed by Chick Hicks. Lightning honorably pushes The King to the finish line, so the respected race car can bow out on a high.

> "You ain't gonna win unless you've got good folks behind you..."

Team player

The King wouldn't have won seven Piston Cups without having a fabulous team around him. From his Dinoco sponsors to his pit crew, they offer The King the loyalty, friendship and darn fast pit stops he values above all else.

Lovely Lynda

The King's wife, Lynda, is the veteran race car's #1 fan. Win or lose, The King is always her champion.

Rear spoiler keeps The King firmly on the racetrack at high speeds

Dinoco logo – the mark of a champion!

Dinoco Blue paint job

CHICK HICKS

ROTTEN RACER Chick Hicks is desperate to win a Piston Cup. He has bumped and cheated his way to more second places than any car in history, always finishing as runner-up to The King. With The King about to retire, Chick is sure this is his chance to be a winner.

Mean green team
Chick's team is the pits. They laugh at Chick's terrible jokes and wear equally terrible moustaches.

Did You Know?
Lightning gives Chick a nickname – "Thunder" – because thunder always comes after lightning!

Hollow victory
Chick finally wins the Piston Cup, but nobody cheers. Everyone has witnessed his dirty tricks and bad sportsmanship and they boo him off the podium.

Chick the chump
Chick Hicks's biggest fan is himself. He believes he is talented, handsome and hilarious. However, only his team and pit crew agree – and that's because he pays them to!

"The Piston Cup – it's mine, dude, it's mine!"

High-visibility advertising space

Beady eyes

Chick's official sponsor: Hostile Takeover Bank

RUSTY AND DUSTY

BROTHERS RUSTY AND Dusty Rust-eze are the joint founders of Rust-eze Medicated Bumper Ointment. They sponsor Lightning McQueen, but he thinks the shabby duo are bad for his hotshot image, despite the fact that they gave him his first big break.

Promotion
Rusty and Dusty host the Rust-eze hospitality tent at races to promote their Medicated Bumper Ointment.

Rusty is literally falling apart

Rust and corrosion on body

Rusty
Rusty is a 1963 Dodge Dart vehicle. He finds even the slightest thing incredibly funny, and so does his brother.

A squirt of Rust-eze is needed!

Large windscreen

Dusty's windows are dusty

Dusty
Dusty is a 1967 Dodge Van. Not content with laughing at his own worn-out jokes, he also enjoys poking fun at Lightning, particularly his car sticker headlights.

"We might even clear enough to buy you some headlights!"

Headlights barely emit light because they are so dusty

IDENTICAL TWINS MIA and Tia are Lightning McQueen's biggest fans. The glamorous groupies cheer him on whenever and wherever they can. The only way to tell these two sisters apart is by their number plates.

Super fans

Mia and Tia go to all of Lightning's races. When he flashes his lucky lightning bolt, they practically faint with excitement!

Retractable hood

Red paint job to match Lightning's

Mia

Mia and her sister Tia are covered in stickers in honour of their hero Lightning. Replica lightning bolts, Lightning's race number 95, and, of course, some heart stickers all show that they are his #1 fans.

Tia is often in awe of Lightning's skills on the racetrack

The twins are adorned with heart stickers

"We love you, Lightning!"

Tia

Mia and Tia prove to be fickle fans. When Lightning goes missing before the final race of the Piston Cup, they switch their allegiance to his rival, Chick Hicks!

THE TUNER GANG

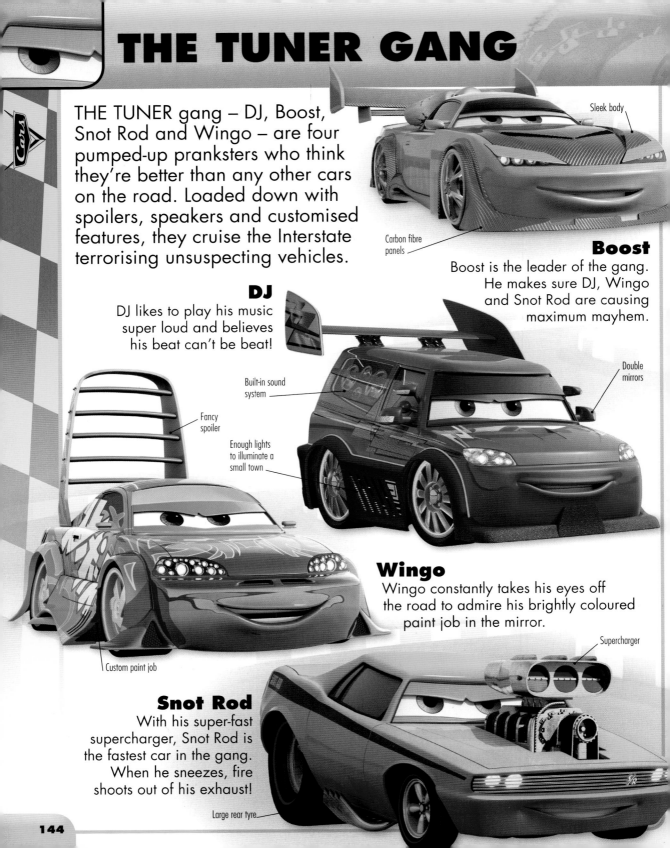

THE TUNER gang – DJ, Boost, Snot Rod and Wingo – are four pumped-up pranksters who think they're better than any other cars on the road. Loaded down with spoilers, speakers and customised features, they cruise the Interstate terrorising unsuspecting vehicles.

Sleek body

Carbon fibre panels

Boost

Boost is the leader of the gang. He makes sure DJ, Wingo and Snot Rod are causing maximum mayhem.

Double mirrors

DJ

DJ likes to play his music super loud and believes his beat can't be beat!

Built-in sound system

Fancy spoiler

Enough lights to illuminate a small town

Wingo

Wingo constantly takes his eyes off the road to admire his brightly coloured paint job in the mirror.

Supercharger

Custom paint job

Snot Rod

With his super-fast supercharger, Snot Rod is the fastest car in the gang. When he sneezes, fire shoots out of his exhaust!

Large rear tyre

TEX

TEX IS A SMOOTH-TALKING Texan and the owner of the mighty oil company, Dinoco. He is honest, honourable and, above all, loyal. Tex holds the keys to the hottest sponsorship deal in racing – every car would love to be a Dinoco race car. He is on the lookout for a successor to The King, who is due to retire.

Good guy
Nice guy Tex is extremely generous. He even lets Lightning's new pal Mater take a ride in his luxury executive helicopter!

Dream sponsor
Tex is used to race cars schmoozing him to try and get the sponsorship that all race cars dream of. The accompanying fame, money and glamorous lifestyle certainly fire up Chick's engine!

Did You Know?
Dinoco's success is down to a hard-working and harmonious team. The King and Tex are great friends and have been together for years.

"You sure made Dinoco proud. Thank you, King."

Dedicated
Tex knows it takes a lot of hard work and dedication to win – he started Dinoco with just one small oil well and it's now the largest oil company in the world! He values loyalty and fair play above instant success.

Metallic gold paint job

FINN MCMISSILE

FINN MCMISSILE is a suave secret agent from British Intelligence. Cool, cunning and charismatic, Finn remains unflappable even in extreme danger. Slick spy skills, plus a stockpile of gadgets, mean that Finn can manoeuvre his way out of the tightest corners and stickiest situations.

Sly spy
Finn is an expert at hiding in the shadows. When he uncovers a plot by Professor Z to disrupt the World Grand Prix, Finn gets ready for the mission of a lifetime.

"I haven't properly introduced myself. Finn McMissile, British Intelligence."

On fire
Finn's rocket launchers are concealed in his headlights. When this secret agent sets his sight on a target, he never misses.

Gadgets galore
Finn's cool collection of gadgets includes rocket launchers, a secret camera and a glass-cutting machine. They are cunningly concealed to make sure enemy agents are taken by surprise!

Tails cut through currents

Tyres extend out for extra flotation

Finn's fins

HOLLEY SHIFTWELL

BRITISH AGENT Holley Shiftwell is fresh out of the secret agent academy. She knows the training manual by heart but has not yet experienced a real mission. When she unexpectedly finds herself working in the field with Finn McMissile, the brave agent shifts up a gear and prepares to face real danger for the first time!

Under pressure
Holley feels under pressure working with top secret agent Finn McMissile. However, she is a hard worker and a fast learner and is sure she can impress the experienced agent with her enthusiasm.

Rear tail extends upward when in flight mode

Secret wings unfold out of side

Holley has a stash of hidden gadgets to surprise the enemy

Gadget geek
High-tech Holley is fitted out with all the latest gadgets and gizmos. She's never used them in the field though, and she can't wait to test them on her first mission.

Rookie no more
Finn has never worked with an agent who has so much high-tech equipment under her hood. But Holley shows him that her gadgets, such as her onboard computer, are invaluable when hunting down the enemy!

SIDDELEY

SIDDELEY IS A slick British secret service jet plane. He spends his time flying other agents on top-secret missions and then dropping them right in the danger zone. Silver-bodied Siddeley is ultra-reliable and incredibly brave, and agents breathe sighs of relief when he swoops in to rescue them!

On approach!
Siddeley comes to Finn and Mater's rescue when they are being attacked by the Lemons. He then flies them and Holley Shiftwell from Tokyo to Paris.

Twin jet engines

Did You Know?
One of Siddeley's close pals is Stephenson, a spy train that takes Finn, Holley and Mater from Paris to Italy.

Sleek body aerodynamically designed to reach super-fast speeds

Techno jet
Siddeley is packed full of the latest state-of-the-art gadgets. With his ultra-powerful twin engine, radar-beating cloaking technology and arsenal of high-tech weapons, he's fine-tuned for the highest performance!

"I'm on approach!"

Come fly with me
Siddeley and Finn McMissile have completed many missions together. Finn trusts Siddeley to always fly to his rescue.

ROD "TORQUE" REDLINE

ROD "TORQUE" REDLINE is an American secret agent and one of the finest in the force. As a muscle car, he has extra strength. However, he is also able to flex other powers, including intelligence, quick wits and the ability to completely change his appearance!

Mission possible

Rod has vital information regarding the plot to sabotage the WGP. He has to pass it on to another agent and nothing, not even a mean Lemon, is going to get in his way!

High pressure

With the bad guys hot on his tail, Rod has no choice but to pass the information to rusty truck Mater. What's the worst that could happen?

Cool customer

Redline is renowned for his ability to stay calm under pressure. Worrying is for wimps and can compromise a mission! Even near his untimely end, when Professor Z threatens him with his secret weapon, Redline continues to insult the Lemons!

His expression hides a calm manner

Did You Know?
Rod is a master of disguises. He is even able to disguise himself as a Lemon car!

Concealed gun

FRANCESCO BERNOULLI

ITALIAN GRAND PRIX champion Francesco Bernoulli is Lightning McQueen's major rival to win the World Grand Prix. Fast, flashy and a total show-off, he is the most successful race car in Europe. But despite Bernoulli's big-mouth bravado, he really respects his rivals and is a good sport.

Attention seeker

Francesco enjoys nothing more than being in the spotlight. When the attention isn't on him, a spin on one of his sleek, 100% Italian Rotelli tyres is sure to get the press bulbs flashing again.

"Francesco is TRIPLE speed!"

Numero uno

Francesco uses sheer power to get ahead of his rivals on the track. But he also has some special tactics to rile his rivals, like teasing.

Francesco's fans

Francesco has a huge following of fans from around the world. They admire his sleek finish and open wheels. The Italian fans love to get behind their hero, particularly when he races at his hometown track of Porta Corsa!

Red, white and green paint job – the colours of the Italian flag

Did You Know?
When Francesco was young, he would sneak into the famous Monza racecourse and practise for hours.

CARLA VELOSO

CARLA VELOSO IS flying the flag for female racers everywhere – she is the only female competing in the World Grand Prix. From Rio De Janeiro, Brazil, the South American superstar car loves to samba. Her sense of rhythm and car-nival spirit help give her both amazing power and superb stamina.

Determined rookie
The World Grand Prix is Carla's first major race. She is determined to put Brazil on the racing map!

Did You Know?
Carla's race number is 8. She set a new track record on her local circuit.

Sight-seeing
Carla feels at home cruising around Japan's streets. They remind her of her home country, Brazil, because of the bright lights and bustling crowds.

Carla's crisis
When Veloso comes third in the Tokyo WGP race, she's on top form. However, in Italy she's hit by Professor Z's secret weapon and her fuel tank explodes. With the London race looming, this puts Carla in a fix. Luckily, she is fully repaired and ready to race in time!

World Grand Prix deco

Detailed design inspired by Car-nival in Brazil

Electric blue hubcaps

MILES AXLEROD

MILES AXLEROD is a filthy rich oil tycoon. However, he appears to have decided to use his powers (and trunkful of money) to make the world a better place. An environmental campaigner, Miles has converted to electricity and is promoting Allinol, a cheap and safe eco-friendly fuel.

Electric dreams
Axlerod used to be a gas guzzler, but now he is customised to within an inch of his life to be environmentally friendly. The wire coils in his wheels are connected to an electric battery, and he even has a solar panel on his roof!

New fuel
Miles creates the World Grand Prix to demonstrate the power of Allinol. All the race cars, including Lightning McQueen, are using it.

"Alternative energy is the future!"

Greedy, not green
Actually, the only green thing about Miles Axlerod is his paint job. The tycoon is more evil than eco-friendly and is behind an elaborate plot to destroy race cars and discredit Allinol forever, so he can get rich from oil again!

Allinol logo is on grille

Green paint job to match green views

Wire coils in wheels are connected to electric battery

PROFESSOR Z

PROFESSOR Z IS a mad scientist with a twisted mind. The monocle-wearing inventor spends his time designing dangerous weapons and hatching dastardly plots. His latest venture is a plot to disrupt the WGP and turn the world against alternative energy, so that cars will rely on gasoline and bring profits to the Lemon cars.

Wicked weapon
Professor Z's deadly electromagnetic radiation ray is disguised as a camera. It might just be the Professor's most brilliant invention yet. However, the mad scientist isn't counting on a rusty tow truck foiling his plan!

First to go
Secret agent Rod "Torque" Redline is the Professor's first victim. The tough agent doesn't stand a chance against his deadly invention.

"Now no one can stop us!"

Evil minions
Professor Z doesn't work alone – he controls a large and loyal army of very bitter Lemons. They are eager to carry out orders for the unhinged Professor, lured by the promise of the spare parts they crave.

A monocle is the trademark of evil geniuses everywhere

The rusty Professor could use a spray of Rust-eze!

153

UNCLE AND MAMA Topolino are Luigi's favourite uncle and aunt. They live in the pretty Italian village of Santa Routina, near Porto Corsa. Uncle Topolino inspired Luigi and Guido to open their own tyre shop, *Casa Della Tyres*, in Radiator Springs!

Welcome!
The Topolinos are full of warmth and wisdom. They prove that Italian hospitality can't be topped when they invite Lightning's entire pit crew to stay.

Soft top

Wise guy
Uncle Topolino is the oldest car in town, but with years of experience under his hood, he's also the wisest! Cars travel for miles to visit Topolino's village tyre shop, to ask for advice on everything from tyres to friendship.

"A wise car hears one word and understands two."

Fiat tyres

Creamy paint job

Elegant whitewall tyres

Full of fuel
Mama Topolino believes the secret to a happy car is a full stomach. She produces the finest fuel in Santa Routina and has made it her mission to make sure the villagers are well fed with her homemade recipe.

VICTOR H

THE LEMON FAMILIES are controlled by powerful Lemonheads. Victor H is head of the Hugo Lemon family. He is in serious need of repair and is known to break down often. But Victor's not worried – he's got a personal chauffeur, Ivan, to tow him around!

"Is the Big Boss here yet?"

V for victory

Victor is a very rich villain. He has made huge amounts of money running a network of corrupt oil refineries. Now that he has worked himself up to the position of Head of the Hugos, he intends to run the crime organisation like the well-oiled machine that he's not.

The help

Tough truck Ivan is not only Victor's chauffeur, he is also his personal bodyguard. However, Ivan is easily distracted, especially if the distraction is a pretty sports car with a flat tyre.

Aggressive expression

Did You Know?

The Lemons are divided into four families, namely the Hugos, Gremlins, Pacers and Trunkovs.

Victor leaks little and often

TOMBER

TINY TOMBER IS a French three-wheeler-dealer. He has a market stall where he sells old spare parts from a variety of sources, but the dubious dealer never reveals where he got them all from. Tomber's name means "to fall" in French. This three-wheeler is sometimes a little unsteady!

Foreign friends
Mater and Tomber hit it off right away. They have mutual respect for each other because of their extensive knowledge of car engines and parts.

Tomber the trader
Tomber is actually one of Finn McMissile's secret informants. The wobbly three-wheeler feeds Finn information on the Lemons and their attempts to get special spare parts.

In the know
Tomber and Finn have worked together for many years. There's nothing this tiny car doesn't know about cars!

Deep concentration

Mirror close to eyes

Two lights to see small spare parts

Unstable wheel

"Are you kidding me?"

GREM AND ACER are Professor Z's chief henchcars. They are both Lemons – members of a global gang of cars with design faults and performance issues. Made bitter by their problems, the Lemons join Professor Z in his scheme to become the most powerful cars in the world.

Lemon head
Acer isn't afraid to do Professor Z's dirty work. Via a headset, he obediently takes orders to blow up the WGP race cars as they speed past.

"Smile for the camera!"

Acer
Rusty and dented, Acer the Pacer has always felt like an outcast in the car world. He isn't afraid to get his wheels dirty by doing Professor Z's evil bidding.

Acer could use a new paint job

Bumper could fall off at any moment

Grem is in serious need of a wash

Grem
Grim Grem is envious of any cars that are polished, sleek and with all their parts intact. The only positive thing about Grem is that he enjoys his work!

Grim, determined expression

SHU TODOROKI

SHU TODOROKI IS A LMP-type race car from Japan. His red and white paint job and Japanese dragon design reflect his proud Japanese heritage. Shu is focused, fierce and flies along at enormous speeds. He grew up at the base of an active volcano, which perhaps explains his fiery personality!

Did You Know?
Shu is a Le Mans Prototype race car. This means that he is custom-built for sports car and endurance racing.

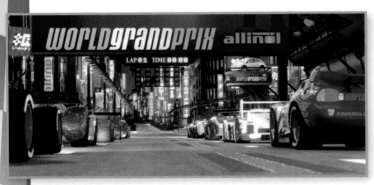

Seven setback
Shu is targeted by the Lemons at the Porta Corsa race and his engine explodes! Despite this setback, strong Shu recovers and makes it to the final race in London.

Winning team
Shu's crew chief, Mach Matsuo, is the only Japanese race car ever to win at Le Mans – a tough 24-hour race in France. So Shu knows he is on the right track to success.

On target
Shu is the Suzaka Champion of Japan, making him a fierce contender at the World Grand Prix. He hopes to prove his champion-level skills and do his home country proud.

Lightweight wing mirror

Legendary red dragon decal

JEFF GORVETTE

JEFF GORVETTE IS an all-American racing hero. His consistent top 10 finishes led to him being crowned Rookie of the Year and means he is a strong entrant into the World Grand Prix. With the Stars and Stripes incorporated into his paint job, this rising star has already earned his stripes!

Stocky build
Jeff Gorvette might not be as streamlined as the other WGP contenders, but his strong body and legendary endurance make him a lethal opponent.

"Can you believe this party?"

Legends
Jeff is well known in the racing world for his awesome accelerating abilities. He is supported by his crew chief, John Lassetire, who is known for his decisive leadership and ability to get the job done.

Grand Gorvette
Jeff Gorvette is a Grand Touring car and always appears as number 24. He's so dedicated to his sport, he moved to Indiana to be closer to the racing action. The move pays off – Gorvette manages to complete all three WGP races, keeping his incredible record intact.

Stars and stripes of American flag

Jeff is on a mission to win the WGP!

JACKSON STORM

JACKSON STORM HAS shaken up the world of racing! This ambitious Next Gen is streamlined for speed. He is confident that nothing will stop him from winning the Piston Cup – not even Lightning McQueen.

Simulator success
Storm trains on a high-tech race simulator instead of on an actual track. He believes that using virtual reality to analyse his performance gives him the edge.

Storming ahead
Storm is all about speed and power, but does he have the real-life race experience to beat Lightning to the Piston Cup?

Rude racer
Storm may be talented, but he has a lot to learn about treating others with respect. The overconfident contender is also obsessed with being in the spotlight.

Confident expression

Did You Know?
Next-generation racers use the latest technology to improve their performance – they are high tech and high speed!

State-of-the-art tyres.

NATALIE CERTAIN

RACER METRIX with NATALIE CERTAIN

TV racing pundit Natalie Certain believes that there's nothing greater than data. The analyst uses her mathematical mind to predict the winner of each race. Many viewers count on her predictions!

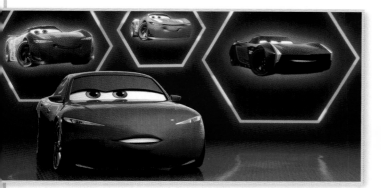

Bitter Chick
Natalie appears on a TV show named *Chick's Picks*. It is presented by Chick Hicks, an old racing rival of Lightning McQueen. These days, the vile veteran uses his show to fire cheap insults at his former nemesis!

"The racing world is changing."

Fact-packed!
Natalie's knowledge of racers is amazing! She's an expert on everything from weight distribution to aerodynamics.

Amazing analytical mind

Number cruncher
Natalie is certain that data is always right. However, her calculations don't take into account the incredible passion that drives champions like Lightning McQueen!

Freshly polished

Dark red paintjob

CRUZ RAMIREZ

Cruz Ramirez is a major factor in the success of the Next Gens. With her quirky coaching methods and instinct for knowing what makes a racer tick, Cruz can turn a rookie into a winner!

Did You Know?
Cruz uses music and pictures to help her racers focus, especially if they are feeling homesick.

Top trainer
Cruz is the best trainer at the Rust-eze Racing Centre – and probably in the country! Her results are incredible, especially for someone so new to the business. She finds the best in each of her racers.

Sterling boss
Cruz's boss, Sterling, knows that she is an important part of the business. She makes racers go faster – which makes him more money.

Full of fun
Training with Cruz is never dull! Her offbeat sense of humour, lively personality and unusual training methods mean that there's often a surprise just around the corner!

"Ready to meet it, greet it and defeat it?"

Each of Cruz's tyres has a name!

Body made of lightweight alloy

MISS FRITTER

Miss Fritter is the fiercest and most feared competitor in the Thunder Hollow Crazy Eight demolition derby. Every week, the battered bus slams her rivals out of the race. She is determined to dent her way to victory!

"Your licence plate's gonna look real nice in my collection."

Fritter time
Anyone attending the demolition derby will hear Miss Fritter's army of rowdy fans. They love to chant, "It's Fritter Time!" whenever she is winning.

Horn-shaped smokestacks

Pile of plates
Miss Fritter loves to hang the number plates of her victims on her side. These trophies terrify the other cars, who wonder whether their plates will be next!

Fritter fears
Miss Fritter will give you the jitters! With her sharp, pointed smokestacks and even sharper insults, she intimidates all who race against her.

Heavy chains to hold her hood down

Serious dents from years of smashing and crashing

SMOKEY

Smokey is famous in racing circles for discovering the Hudson Hornet. An amazing crew chief and mentor, Smokey turned a rookie into a champion! These days, Smokey is retired from racing, but he has a lot of wisdom to pass on to others.

"Funny what a racer can do when he's not overthinking things."

Proud mentor
Smokey shows Lightning letters from Doc Hudson. They show how much Doc loved being McQueen's coach. This gives Lightning a new perspective on his old friend.

Training with Smokey
When Smokey comes out of retirement to coach Lightning McQueen, he uses old-school training methods tried and tested over the years. No simulators allowed! As part of his program, Smokey arranges for bales of hay to be thrown at Lightning!

1946 Hudson pickup truck

Brown paint finish

Smokey's garage logo

THE LEGENDS

In the 1950s, a generation of pioneering racers like the Hudson Hornet emerged, making it a magical time for the sport. Each of these Legends has some incredible stories to tell, and they are happy to share them with the track stars of today.

Junior Moon

Junior "Midnight" Moon took a shine to racing through the woods at night, then turned to the track full time. These days Junior is more senior, but his unique spirit and winning spark have never waned.

Steel body work

Headlights (that he doesn't use under a full moon)

River Scott

River Scott is one of the great battlers of racing. He rose from humble beginnings to the dizzy heights of the Piston Cup. His racing style was never graceful, each win earning him a few dents along the way!

Oversized dirt track tyres

"Once we got on the track, we didn't want to leave."

Louise Nash

Louise Nash

Louise "Barnstormer" Nash was the first female to make it big in Piston Cup racing. As well as beating old-fashioned attitudes, she beat most of the other racers, too.

Louise keeps herself in top condition

REMY

RATS AREN'T supposed to like humans, and they certainly aren't supposed to have a passion for cooking. But Remy isn't like other rats, who spend their time eating rubbish, dodging traps and avoiding poison. Remy has a special talent, and he dreams of being a famous chef just like his hero, Auguste Gusteau.

Nosing around

Remy has a highly developed sense of smell and taste. These skills help to make him a great chef, but they are also pretty useful skills for a rat. Remy is the best poison-checker in the whole colony.

Lucky break

Remy's curiosity about humans leads to trouble, just as his dad said it would. The rat colony has to flee its home, thanks to Remy, while he ends up alone in Paris. Fortunately, he finds himself right outside Gusteau's restaurant!

> "If you are what you eat, then I only want to eat the good stuff."

Sensitive nose

Anyone can cook

When the food critic Anton Ego demands dinner, Remy knows just what to make – ratatouille. After a single bite, the famous critic is a changed man and declares that Remy is "the finest chef in France".

Hygienically clean paws

Natural chef

At first, Remy's pal Linguini gets all the credit for being the exciting new chef. When the truth is revealed, it takes a while for everyone to get used to the idea, but with a pinch of luck, a dollop of friendship and a *soupçon* of talent, Remy finally finds the recipe for success.

LINGUINI

Did You Know?
Linguini has been fired from every job he has ever had. Working at *Gusteau's* is his last chance.

WHEN CLUMSY garbage boy Linguini spills the soup in *Gusteau's* kitchen, it turns out to be the luckiest accident he has ever had. Remy saves the soup and Linguini's job, and the unlikely pair form a double act that will change both of their lives.

In control
Linguini has a problem: He can't actually cook, but Remy can. Clever Remy has an idea – he hides under Linguini's chef's hat and guides his movements by pulling his hair. Amazingly, it works!

Ill-fitting chef's uniform

Food of love
It's not always fun being controlled by a rat, but Linguini finds some unexpected benefits. Not only does the "little chef" take control in the kitchen, he also gives his shy pal a head start with his love life.

> "You know how to cook, and I know how to appear human."

An heir in the soup
Linguini is Auguste Gusteau's secret son, but he has none of his father's talent. However, when Remy's soup is a hit, Linguini gets the credit and is asked to make it all over again. With Remy's help, Linguini is a success.

True chums
Taking a chance on a talented rat is the smartest thing Linguini has ever done. His life has never been better!

Beat-up old trainers

SKINNER

SNEAKY CHEF Skinner is a small guy with big plans. After Chef Gusteau's death, he becomes Head Chef and doesn't let anyone forget who's boss. The short-tempered chef rules the kitchen by fear. However, when he meets an even smaller chef, Skinner finally gets what he deserves.

Ratting them out
Linguini and Remy are too smart for Skinner, but the mean chef has the last laugh. He reports the rat infestation to the health inspector, and *Gusteau's* is closed down!

"You're fired!"

Large toque (chef's hat)

Mean expression

Short-term thinking
Skinner only cares about making money, so he wants to put *Gusteau's* name on a tacky range of fast food. The great Auguste Gusteau would be horrified!

Sneaky
Until Linguini arrives, Chef Skinner stands to inherit the restaurant. He is determined that Linguini will not find out that he is really Gusteau's son.

Aggressive stance

Low-down chef
Scheming Skinner smells a rat. He knows that Linguini is hiding one somewhere, but he can't prove it. When he finally works out that the rat is the chef, Skinner kidnaps Remy and tries to make him create a range of frozen fast food for him.

Short legs

Did You Know?
Vertically challenged Chef Skinner is obsessed with looking taller. He wears an extra-large chef's hat, but still needs a ladder to taste the soup!

COLETTE

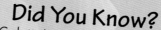

AS THE ONLY female chef working at *Gusteau's*, Colette has had to be tough to survive. She is often the first person to arrive in the morning and the last one to leave at night. She is determined to be a top chef. But underneath her hard-baked exterior, Colette is sweet and kind.

Getting fresh
Colette can tell if a loaf of bread is fresh just by tapping it. To her, a fresh loaf sounds like sweet music!

Spotless white uniform

Busy hands

Follow the recipe!
Colette always follows Gusteau's original recipes to the letter. She truly believes in his motto that anyone can cook – even the garbage boy. Or a rat!

"You are one of us now."

Tough teacher
Colette is assigned to teach rookie chef Linguini the basics. At first, she is very strict, but as Linguini proves to be a willing and grateful pupil, Colette starts to like him. And when he kisses her (thanks to Remy, of course), she starts to do more than just like him...

Standing up for others
Colette has strong principles and stands up for what, and whom, she believes in.

Sensible, nonslip shoes

EMILE

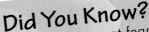

Did You Know?
Emile has two great fears in life – being hungry, and being struck by lightning!

REMY'S BIG BROTHER is a picky eater – whatever he picks up, he eats. Emile is happy to eat rubbish and doesn't understand Remy's love of fine food or his habit of washing his paws before eating. However, easygoing Emile accepts that his brother is different and goes along with all his ideas, no matter how weird or dangerous they are!

Caught!
For once, Emile is not thinking about food. Thanks to his little brother, he is in danger of being shot by a little old lady!

"You have a gift!"

Greedy rat
Remy's new job is a dream come true for Emile, who goes crazy in the larder.

Cheerful smile

A handy snack

Teamwork
The two brothers have very different goals in life – Remy wants to cook food and Emile just wants to eat it – but they are the best of friends.

Full belly

Big brother
Emile loves food, but he loves his brother more. He is the only one who knows about Remy's interest in the world of humans and his dream to become a chef. The two brothers share all of their secrets – well, they would, if Emile had any!

DJANGO

REMY'S DAD HAS no problem with the way rats live or what they eat. To Django, taking food isn't stealing, if nobody wants it. As the rat colony's leader, it is his job to keep the pack together and safe from the rats' greatest enemy – humans. If only he could make his youngest son understand that he is just trying to protect him.

Food advice
Django thinks that being fussy about food is a recipe for disaster. He worries that a sensitive rat like Remy won't survive in the real world. Food is fuel, nothing more.

Protective dad
Django loves both his sons, but Remy is definitely more high-maintenance. Django worries that his youngest son is putting himself and their colony in danger by getting caught up in the world of humans. After all, what's so wrong with being a rat?

"Shut up and eat your garbage!"

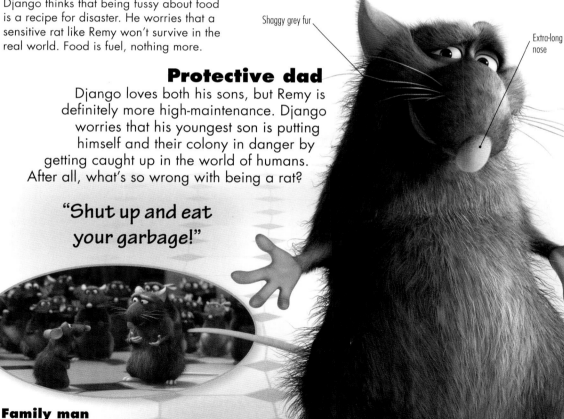

Shaggy grey fur

Extra-long nose

Family man
Django doesn't agree with Remy's career choices, but when his son needs help, he is there for him. If Remy needs some kitchen staff, then Django and his colony will scrub up and pitch in!

GUSTEAU

ONCE CONSIDERED the finest chef in Paris, Auguste Gusteau ran a five-star restaurant, wrote a world-famous cookbook and also starred in his own TV cooking show. Unfortunately, a bad review of his restaurant by food critic Anton Ego cost Gusteau one of his stars and broke the now four-star chef's heart.

Bright lights
Before Ego's review, *Gusteau's* was the most fashionable restaurant in Paris and was fully booked five months in advance.

Anyone can cook
Auguste Gusteau was the youngest chef ever to get a five-star rating. But despite being a culinary genius, he believed that creativity could come from anyone, anywhere. His cookbook, *Anyone Can Cook,* is budding chef Remy's most cherished possession.

Extra-slim chef's hat

"Anyone can cook, but only the fearless can be great."

Ghostly white chef uniform

Did You Know?
When Gusteau died, his restaurant lost another one of its stars. The now three-star restaurant is a shadow of its former glory.

Friend in need
Alone in Paris, Remy could really use a friend. Somehow, the spirit of Chef Gusteau appears to guide him. Is he real? Remy doesn't know, but, real or not, he helps the talented rat believe in himself.

ANTON EGO

THE WORLD'S most feared food critic loves to dish out cutting criticisms. Ego's reviews can make or break a chef's reputation, but the fussy foodie is extremely hard to please and few restaurants ever meet his high standards. He is an expert on fine food, but doesn't seem to find much pleasure in eating it.

Long, bony fingers

Did You Know?
Ego has a loyal butler named Ambritser. The poor man is terrified of his brooding boss.

Food snob
Ego's beliefs are the complete opposite of Gusteau's. The culinary connoisseur does not believe that just anyone can cook. Certainly not a rat!

Hard to please
Remy and Linguini are creating a sensation in *Gusteau's* kitchen, but their success brings an unwelcome visitor – Anton Ego. The cranky critic demands to be hit with Linguini's "best shot". He doesn't expect to be impressed.

Happy memories
One bite of Remy's ratatouille, and Anton Ego's cold heart melts. His big ego disappears as he remembers a little Ego whose mother comforted him with simple food, seasoned with love.

Long, skinny legs

"I take cooking very seriously."

A new Anton
Eating Remy's food changes Anton Ego forever. He becomes a happier person and learns to really love food again.

THE CHEFS

A GOOD KITCHEN requires organisation, teamwork and a certain *je ne sais quoi* – and *Gusteau's* is no exception. Although Skinner is the boss, it is his highly trained, highly skilled and highly unusual chefs who do all the really hard work.

Did You Know?

Fish Chef Lalo ran away from home to be an acrobat, until he decided he preferred cooking.

Lalo – Fish Chef

Pompidou – Pastry Chef

Many hands

There's always something to do in the kitchen: peeling, chopping, slicing, dicing, roasting and toasting. And the hard work isn't over when the food is cooked. Then, the dirty dishes have to be washed!

The food chain

Every chef in the kitchen has a different specialty, and they all work together to create gourmet meals to order. The chefs have to be talented and tough to survive in *Gusteau's* kitchen.

Horst – Assistant Head Chef

Did You Know?

Horst claims to have been in prison. It was either for fraud, bank robbery or making a hole in the ozone layer. He can't decide!

Larousse – Salad and Appetiser Chef

MUSTAFA

AS HEAD WAITER at *Gusteau's*, Mustafa is one of the most important people working in the restaurant. The chefs might think that the hard work happens in the kitchen, but it is Mustafa and his team of waiters who must ensure that customers have a first-rate dining experience.

New creations
Linguini and Remy's success in the kitchen means that customers are demanding new, exciting dishes. And it's up to Mustafa to tell the chefs!

Rat!
When Mustafa grabs a dish from a passing cart, he gets a little more than he expected. Fortunately, Remy is too quick for him.

Tired eyes

Flushed cheeks

"*Do you know what you'd like this evening, sir?*"

Middle man
Plump Mustafa might look like he knows a lot about food, but he just serves it. If things go wrong in the kitchen, it is poor Mustafa who must explain things to the hungry customers. Being a head waiter is a very stressful job!

WALL·E

IT'S 2805, AND humans have left Earth covered in rubbish to live in luxury spaceships. Alone in a world covered in garbage, rusty but reliable WALL•E is the last clean-up unit on Earth. His job is to collect and cube rubbish, but he brightens up his days by discovering treasures among the debris and listening to his favourite song.

Trash to treasure
WALL•E loves to collect artifacts the human race left behind – even if he has no idea what they were actually used for.

Fantastic find
When WALL•E finds a living plant, he has no real idea of what it is. However, he senses that it is precious and is determined to look after it.

Eyes work like binoculars

Extendable neck

Did You Know?
When WALL•E shuts down, he pulls in all his limbs and goes into cube mode. This is also useful when he is scared!

Game changer
The arrival of probe-bot EVE opens WALL•E up to a whole new world. When he shows his new friend the tiny green plant he has found, it triggers events that alter not only WALL•E's destiny, but also that of the entire human race.

Narrow escape
When WALL•E is helping EVE, he is blind to personal peril. He narrowly escapes being destroyed in the exploding escape pod – but saves the vital plant.

Hands to lift and sort rubbish

Treads help WALL•E move around on trash-covered terrain

EVE

COOL, SMART and state-of-the-art, this probe-bot is totally focused on her directive to discover plant life on Earth – until she meets WALL•E. It's not love at first sight for EVE, but the rusty robot soon brings fun, affection and even a little dancing into her super-efficient world.

Light up my life
WALL•E shows how much he cares for EVE by sharing with her the most magical thing in his whole collection.

Shutdown
As soon as EVE sees WALL•E's plant, she shuts down. WALL•E fears that he has lost his new friend forever.

Eyes convey a variety of expressions

Dream team
Returning to space, EVE seems to forget her new friend, until she realises that she needs him. EVE and WALL•E team up against bad bots Auto and GO-4 to save the planet and finally allow humans to go home to Earth.

Sleek body

Arms function like wings

Daring duo
Two bots are better than one when it comes to outwitting the security forces on board the *Axiom*. EVE provides flight power and WALL•E has a never-give-up attitude.

AUTO

THE *AXIOM'S* autopilot is programmed to handle the running of the ship, leaving very little for the human captain to do. The automated steering wheel has a beady red eye that sees everything, making his master feel pretty much useless most of the time.

Who's the boss?
The Captain thinks he calls the shots on the *Axiom* – but when it's crunch time, Auto is ready to confine his "master" to his quarters.

Secret orders
This sneaky robot has a secret: in the case of life ever being found on Earth, it must follow directive "A113", and prevent humans from returning home. The autopilot is programmed to do anything – even disobey the Captain – to carry out his orders.

No way home
Auto is convinced there is no possibility of returning to Earth – but the secret information he relies on is over 700 years out of date.

All-seeing eye

Did You Know?
Auto isn't really a bad guy – he's programmed to follow orders, and there's nothing he can do about it!

Manual override
The mutinous machine has one weakness, and the Captain finally finds it. By switching control to manual, he puts mankind back in charge of its own destiny.

Steering wheel

"Give me the plant."

GO-4

THE HEAD OF security on the *Axiom*, this ruthless little machine knows everything that goes on aboard the ship. He gives the steward-bots their orders and acts swiftly to send any renegade robots to the Repair Ward. GO-4 takes his responsibilities seriously and enjoys any opportunity to fire his red ray at trouble-makers.

Did You Know?
GO-4 ends up taking a trip out of the window of the Control Deck and lands in a heap on the Lido deck!

Self-destruct
Faced with orders to destroy the plant immediately, GO-4 sneaks it into an escape pod and sets it to self-destruct. Luckily, WALL•E is watching!

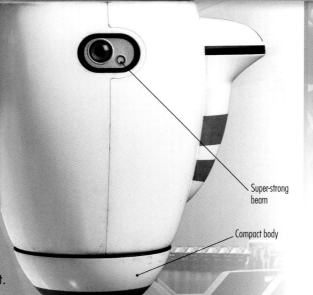

Glowing head

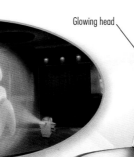

Ray power
He may only be a little guy, but GO-4 can make a big impact with his red ray. It creates a force-field that can even hold back an angry EVE.

Super-strong beam

Compact body

Plant pilferer
GO-4 is not a bad bot, but he has been programmed by the Buy-n-Large Corporation to destroy any vegetation arriving from Earth. He intercepts the plant as soon as EVE arrives, and only WALL•E's heroics prevent GO-4 from destroying it.

M-O

KEEPING THE SHIP clean is all M-O cares about. He is the best in the business, able to spot contamination that humans can't even see. A rotating device attached to his arms can clean away all known dirt in a matter of seconds. Life for M-O is neat and tidy – until he meets WALL•E.

Did You Know?
M-O's name is short for Microbe-Obliterator, and he is programmed to destroy all dirt.

"Foreign contaminant!"

On the trail
Diligent M-O is determined to track WALL•E's trail of contamination to its source and clean up the mess once and for all. Somewhere along the way, his disgust turns to respect for a robot that can survive with all that filth.

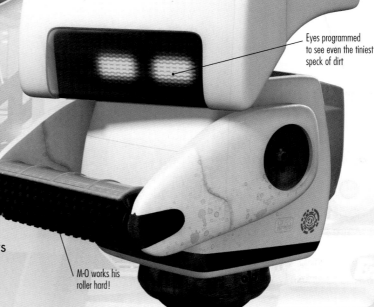

Good, clean fun
Even when the pair have become friends, the dedicated M-O can't resist giving his pal a little polish.

Friend or foe
The new arrival from Earth creates filth readings that go right off the chart. Well, he has spent his whole life working with trash. M-O is so intrigued by WALL•E's dirtiness that he follows the intruder around and even ends up saving his life.

Eyes programmed to see even the tiniest speck of dirt

M-O works his roller hard!

IT WOULD BE hard to find a more motivated worker on the *Axiom* than this Basic Utility Repair Nano Engineer, or BURN•E. The little repair-bot runs on a single track outside the ship and has a single-minded attitude toward getting the job done. Whether it's a humdrum light fixing or major outside repairs, BURN•E is on the case.

WALL•E

Protective eye shield

Hot stuff
BURN•E is an expert welder, and repairing this exterior lamp on the *Axiom* really ought to be a trouble-free job. Unless WALL•E happens to be in the area…

Welder

Light to show the way

Locked out
Not every repair job goes completely to plan, however, and sometimes BURN•E can be a little accident prone. He can be unlucky, too, such as when he is locked outside the ship by WALL•E and EVE after their space flight. Luckily, BURN•E has just the tools to cut his way back in.

Track runner

BEING IN CHARGE of an executive starliner may sound like a stressful job, but life is easy for Captain B. McCrea. The ship is run by robots, so all he has to do is greet the passengers every morning and remind them what day it is. He gives a daily weather report: It's always a pleasant 72 degrees!

Groomed to go

The Captain is so reliant on machine pampering, he simply cannot face the day without his massage from a HAN-S bot and grooming by a PR-T bot.

Captain's hat

Plump face

Did You Know?

In 2805, humans have grown so pampered and lazy that they move around on hover chairs and interact with each other using holo-screens.

"I don't want to survive. I want to live."

I'm in charge!

The Captain proves that he is the man in charge when evidence arrives that the Earth is habitable again. He defies the orders of the BnL corporation (and his own autopilot) to launch a daring bid to take the human race home. But first, he'll have to practise using his legs again...

Epaulette denotes rank

Precious plant

JOHN AND MARY

PAMPERED PASSENGERS on the *Axiom*, John and Mary have drifted out of the habit of doing things for themselves, just like the rest of mankind. However, chance encounters with WALL•E wake them both up out of their stupor. When the pair meet up, they begin to enjoy life again.

Down to earth
When the *Axiom* finally returns to Earth, John and Mary are there to witness the beginning of a new life. They share the moment when the Captain plants the first green shoot.

Meet WALL•E
John thinks WALL•E must be a drink-bot when he first bumps into him. In fact, he tumbles right out of his chair trying to hand over his empty cup.

Did You Know?
Passengers like John and Mary have no need to buy new clothes. They just touch a screen and their day-suits change colour instantly.

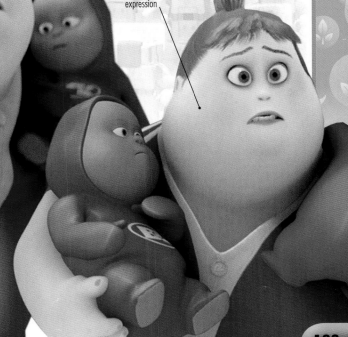

Typical human outfit

Surprised expression

New outlook
When John bumps into Mary, the two make an instant connection. They become so reenergised that when Auto tries to take control of the *Axiom*, John and Mary join forces to save the humans on board.

BOTS

THE 5,000 passengers on board the *Axiom* are served by 500,000 robots. Whether they need a massage, a haircut or even a game of golf, there is a bot, or several, who will do it for them. Thanks to the bots, humans don't have to do a thing for themselves.

STEWARD-BOTS
Created to maintain order on the ship, steward-bots patrol the decks looking for signs of trouble.

HAN-S
This massage-bot offers a stimulating facial or a soothing back-rub.

L-T
A mobile lamp will follow passengers anywhere they need to go.

VQ-M
Part of the cleaning team, the vacuum-bot scans the *Axiom* for minute dust particles.

PR-T
This beautician-bot is armed with lipstick, scissors, powder-puffs, tweezers and much more.

BUF-R
Buffer-bots polish the *Axiom* paintwork to a shiny sheen.

DRINK-BOT
These eager servants are programmed to detect signs of thirst.

REPAIR-BOT
Repair-bots can be found all over the ship, quietly keeping things working.

SPRAY-BOT
Each spray-bot is equipped with anti-bacterial spray to keep the *Axiom* squeaky clean.

NAN-E
These bots deliver lessons in maths and literacy. They can also change nappies in a crisis.

FOOD DISPENSER-BOT
Delivering meals straight to passengers' hover-chairs, these waiters can also display a picture menu on their screens.

TENNIS-BOT
The tennis-bot doesn't need a partner – it will happily play itself.

COCKROACH

THIS TOUGH LITTLE insect is a natural survivor, just like his friend WALL•E. They have been companions a long time and just seem to know how to get along. It's lucky the cockroach has a tough shell, as WALL•E often runs over it with his heavy treads.

Bug buddy
The cockroach is special to WALL•E, as it seems to be the only thing that shares an otherwise lifeless world with him. The robot always takes time out of his chores to check up on his tiny pal.

Patient pal
WALL•E knows his trip into space is going to be dangerous, so he makes sure his insect friend stays behind. On the robot's return, the cockroach is right where WALL•E left him.

Did You Know?
Cockroaches have amazing powers of survival. Many experts believe that they will remain on Earth if humans become extinct!

Long feelers

Loyal roach
This friendly bug helps bring WALL•E and EVE together when the robots are too shy to make the first move. The cockroach is a loyal creature and can be relied upon to stay home and stay safe while WALL•E heads off on his incredible adventure.

WALL•E's comeback
When EVE returns a damaged WALL•E to Earth, the cockroach shares her concern for his old friend. While EVE struggles to fix WALL•E, the loyal insect anxiously watches every step of the process.

Extra-tough wings

CARL FREDRICKSEN

IT'S HARD to imagine that grouchy Carl Fredricksen was once a small boy with dreams of becoming an explorer. But when a construction company tries to force him out of his house and into a retirement home, Carl hatches an exciting plan. He is off on an adventure – to South America's Paradise Falls!

"Cross my heart"

Carl's first encounter with future wife Ellie ended with a broken arm and a promise that he'd take her to Paradise Falls one day. With Ellie gone, Carl decides to take their house instead!

"Oh, Ellie, what have I gotten myself into?"

Grape soda badge

Old-fashioned glasses

Hearing aid

Explorer Carl

Carl may be slower than he used to be, but he's certainly no less determined. By hook or by crook, he'll get himself – and his new friends – to safety.

Well-loved armchair

Ready to rebel

Faced with losing his house, Carl imagines what Ellie would do. She sure wouldn't sit in an armchair, doing nothing. Inspired, Carl takes control of his life. His house and memories mean far more to him than obeying the rules.

ELLIE FREDRICKSEN

AS A CHILD, Ellie was determined, talkative and a total tomboy. It was love at first sight for shy Carl. When Ellie told him her plans for the future, he promised that one day, they would go to Paradise Falls. However, after they got married, life got in the way and the couple never realised their dream.

Cheerful smile

"Thanks for the adventure – now go have a new one."

Paintbrush

Sweet dreams
Young Ellie recorded all the things she wanted to do in her precious Adventure Book. She showed it to Carl, because he shared her love of adventure.

Paint-splattered shirt

A lifelong dream
Ellie and Carl both worked at the local zoo. They saved for their Paradise Falls trip in a special jar. But whenever they got near their goal, everyday emergencies, such as fixing the car or repairing the roof, wiped out their savings. When Carl was finally able to buy the plane tickets, it was too late. Ellie was dying.

Happy couple
Before she passed away, Ellie wanted Carl to know that their life together had been enough of an adventure.

Retro outfit

Did You Know?
When Ellie and Carl first met, she gave him a badge made out of a grape soda bottle cap, which he still wears.

RUSSELL

ENERGETIC AND chatty, Russell is a Junior Wilderness Explorer, but he is desperate to become a Senior Wilderness Explorer. All that stands between him and his goal is the Assisting the Elderly badge. When he tries to assist the elderly Mr Fredricksen, Russell gets a lot more than he bargained for!

Wilderness Explorer cap

Snipe-catching net

A badge too far
Tracking a pesky snipe bird for Mr Fredricksen, Russell ends up under the house – and then up in the air. Carl is certainly surprised to hear Russell's knock on the door.

"The wilderness must be explored!"

Tribe 54 kerchief

Real adventurer
Like all Wilderness Explorers, Russell is a keen animal lover. He is determined to protect the bird he's named "Kevin", and also recognises that Dug will be a loyal pet.

Good friends
The best moments in life, Russell and Carl discover, don't have to be wild adventures. They can be as ordinary as sharing an ice cream and counting cars.

KEVIN

WHEN Russell names the giant, colourful bird, he has no idea that "Kevin" is, in fact, female. Kevin spends her time trying to find food for her hungry chicks and trying to avoid capture by Charles F. Muntz's dogs. A chocoholic, Kevin also gobbles up Carl's walking stick and one of his helium balloons!

Long neck

Motherly instinct

Kevin likes Russell instantly, and not just because his pockets are full of chocolate. Missing her chicks, she is glad to have someone to mother. She tosses Russell into the air and rocks him back and forth.

Brightly coloured plumage

Shoo!

Having finally tracked her down, Dug wants to take Kevin prisoner. The problem is, she's twice his size!

Permanently hungry belly

Kevin's chicks

Like their mum, the cheeky chicks will try to eat anything. They slobber all over Carl's stick, so he decides to leave it behind.

Large, clawed feet

Up for fun

Kevin is unlike any other bird. Despite her size, she loves playing hide-and-seek. She dodges behind rocks when she's trying to tag along after Russell and Carl, and then cleverly hides from Muntz among the balloons on Carl's house.

Did You Know?

Kevin is 3.66 metres (12 feet) tall. She lives with her babies inside a maze of twisty rocks called a labyrinth.

DUG

IT'S NOT HARD to love Dug – he is loyal, energetic and completely adorable. He looks like a regular pet but, like all of Charles F. Muntz's dogs, he wears a collar that translates his thoughts into speech. Dug may not be the brightest dog in Muntz's pack, but he is a terrific tracker.

Did You Know?
Mean Alpha makes Dug wear the Cone of Shame to punish him when he loses Kevin.

"I've just met you and I love you."

Peekaboo!
Dug is half Golden Retriever, half Husky. It takes him a while to work out what's going on, but he gets there in the end. One day, he will be top dog!

A dog's life
Position in the pack is everything. That's why Dug is so eager to make a success of tracking Kevin – and why he hates having to admit that he let her get away.

Sensitive nose

Chosen master
Even loyal Dug can see that Carl will be a kinder master than Charles F. Muntz. Puppy-dog eyes won't win over the old man, but bravery in times of danger will.

Ever-wagging tail

Special collar

Perfect pet
All Dug is interested in is being liked – and squirrels. When Russell and Carl first encounter him, they can't believe their ears – a talking dog! Russell begs Carl to keep Dug as their pet.

CHARLES F. MUNTZ

AS ONE OF the world's most famous explorers, Charles F. Muntz travelled the globe in his *Spirit of Adventure* airship discovering rare plants and animals. He was a hero to every young adventurer, including Carl and Ellie. However, one ill-fated trip to Paradise Falls costs Muntz his reputation.

Unshakable fury
Ignoring his creaking limbs, Muntz battles with Carl in his trophy room. Then, determined not to let Carl get away, Muntz scales the exterior of the airship.

Battered leather flight jacket

Aggressive pose

Cold eyes

"Grey leader? Take down the house."

Phony!
When Muntz showed off the skeleton of a giant bird, the scientific world rejected him as a fraud.

Walking stick, or weapon?

Bird-brained
Years of fruitless searching for the mysterious giant bird have left Muntz a bitter man. Utterly obsessed, he'll stop at nothing to find his prize. However, to his dismay, an old man and a small boy beat him to it!

Did You Know?
No one believed that Muntz had really seen a giant bird, so his membership with the National Explorer's Society was withdrawn.

ALPHA

AS HIS NAME suggests, Alpha is the leader of Muntz's pack of dogs. Ferocious and fierce, Alpha is a Doberman who loves being in control. The problem comes when his collar malfunctions – the other dogs find it hard to respect Alpha when his voice is so high and squeaky!

"You two shall have much rewardings from Master for the toil factor you wage."

Confused canines
Alpha's fond of using long, complicated sentences. That's all very well, but it sometimes leaves the pack baffled.

Hyper-sensitive ears

Mean eyes

Super snarler
Even when his voice sounds silly, Alpha can still be frightening. He makes poor Dug cower when he tells him off for losing the bird.

Malfunctioning collar

Bird hunter
Alpha prides himself on his superb tracking skills, yet he has failed to hunt down one of those giant birds that his master, Muntz, is so desperate to find. With his pointy ears and sensitive nose, it can only be a matter of time – can't it?

BETA AND GAMMA

ALPHA'S TRUSTED lieutenants are Beta, a beefy Rottweiler, and Gamma, a strong and sturdy Bulldog. They are stronger than the other members of the pack, and also slightly more intelligent. But only slightly.

Knowing their place
Alpha doesn't like Beta and Gamma laughing at his malfunctioning voice – he worries they might challenge his position. Beta defuses the situation by turning the conversation back around to Dug.

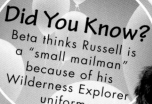

Did You Know?
Beta thinks Russell is a "small mailman" because of his Wilderness Explorer uniform.

Scared expression

Gamma the pilot
Muntz has trained some of his dogs to fly specially designed planes. Gamma controls his plane by biting the bone-shaped joystick.

"Oh, man, Master will not be pleased."

Special collar

Top trackers
Beta and Gamma help Alpha to track down Kevin and her new human pals. Their powerful senses of smell even pick up the scent of the chocolate in Russell's pocket – and Carl's denture cream.

Large paws

KING FERGUS

BIG, BRAVE King Fergus is a loving husband and father, and a kind ruler. His strength and courage once united the clans and brought peace to the Highlands. Now trouble is brewing in Fergus's own castle, and that peace is under threat.

Bear escape
King Fergus lost a leg in a famous battle with the demon bear, Mor'du. He'd love a chance to pay the bear back – and turn the beast into a rug!

Flaming red, curly hair

"Princess or not, learning to fight is essential."

Warm fur cloak

Old warrior
Fun-loving Fergus has a great sense of humour and always lives in the moment. He likes hunting, brawling and eating huge dinners. When he thinks a bear is attacking his family, the King shows his tough side.

DunBroch tartan kilt

Wooden leg

Did You Know?
Fergus is a pretty easy-going guy, except when it comes to bears. He is determined to find Mor'du and protect his family.

QUEEN ELINOR

GRACIOUS QUEEN Elinor rules the kingdom with calm diplomacy. She is the perfect complement to her husband and together the king and queen keep the kingdom peaceful. However, there is one person that Elinor cannot seem to get along with – her daughter.

Simple crown, inlaid with jade

"The clans must know that the DunBrochs honour our commitments."

BRAVE

Traditional tapestry
Elinor stitched this tapestry. It symbolises the love that binds her family together – until Merida rips it.

Regal pose

Tough lesson
Queen Elinor can't understand her daughter's point of view: getting married is Merida's royal duty, so why won't she do it? However, spending some time as a bear helps Elinor to understand how Merida is feeling and the troubled mother and daughter finally reconnect.

Mum-Bear
Merida just wants to change her mother's mind, but a spell changes her body too. Queen Elinor becomes a bear, and it is up to Merida to break the spell before King Fergus starts hunting his wife!

Elegant green gown

PRINCESS MERIDA

FREE-SPIRITED MERIDA is certainly not her mother's idea of a perfect princess. Merida's favourite things are archery, sword fighting and exploring the wild lands around her home, the Kingdom of DunBroch.

"I want my freedom."

Daddy's girl
Merida has inherited her red hair and her love of adventure from her father, King Fergus. He gave Merida her first bow when she was a wee girl and loves to practise swordplay with her.

Trusty bow

Quiver of arrows

Unruly red hair

Did You Know?
Merida is desperate to change her mother's mind – she will try anything, even a spell from a witch.

Steady steed
Merida's horse, Angus, has been her best friend since he was a foal. She can tell him anything and he loves to be part of her adventures.

Taking charge
Merida chooses an archery contest to decide her suitor, then wins it herself! Her mum is angry because Merida's actions inadvertently threaten peace in the kingdom. It is up to Merida to make things right again.

Mom trouble
Lately, Merida and her mum can't seem to get along. Queen Elinor thinks that Merida should get married, but Merida isn't ready for it.

THE TRIPLETS

MERIDA MIGHT NOT be the ideal princess, but her three younger brothers are trouble. Tripled! Princes Harris, Hamish and Hubert are lovable little scamps who spend their time inventing new pranks to play on the unsuspecting inhabitants of the castle.

Big sis
The DunBroch children all have the same red curls and sense of fun. Harris, Hamish and Hubert love to tease their big sister, but help her out when it counts.

Did You Know?
Each triplet always knows what the others are thinking, without words. They don't really need to speak to other people.

Mischievous expression

Familiar red hair

Three little bears
Getting into trouble is hungry work and the triplets are always looking for snacks. When they see the remains of a magical cake, they gobble it right up.

Family tartan

Royal trio
Being turned into bears doesn't bother the mischievous triplets one little bit. In fact, they quite like it! The three royal bears help their sister save their mum, and play a few new tricks as well...

THE WITCH AND MOR'DU

A MYSTERIOUS WITCH lives in the forest. She calls herself a wood-carver, but she knows an awful lot about magic spells that turn people into bears – like the dangerous Mor'du. The demon bear is said to roam the Highlands, striking out at anyone who gets in his way.

Spell cake
Merida thinks that the Witch's cake will solve her problems with her mother, but she needs to listen to her words, too.

Talkative black crow

Shabby green cape

The Witch

The only way to get to the Witch's cottage is with the help of mysterious forest spirits called will o' the wisps. It means that the old lady doesn't get a lot of company, but those who do seek her out always seem to need her help with something big.

Evil eyes

Terrifying teeth

Did You Know?
Mor'du attacked Fergus, Elinor and Merida at a family picnic. It was before the triplets were even born.

Mor'du

Mor'du was once a prince who asked the Witch for a spell to grant him the strength of 10 men. The prince got his wish, but it wasn't exactly what he wanted – the spell turned him into a bear.

YOUNG MACGUFFIN
AND LORD MACGUFFIN

CLAN MACGUFFIN lives in the rainy coastal area of Scotland and speaks in a strongly accented dialogue that is difficult for other people to understand. Lord MacGuffin is the leader of this clan and his strong son is set to follow in his father's footsteps.

My boy
Lord MacGuffin is proud of his strapping son and hopes that he will one day become a strong leader, just like him.

BRAVE

Young MacGuffin

He might be brave on the battlefield, but when it comes to speaking in public, Young MacGuffin is completely tongue-tied. However, it doesn't really matter what the shy young man says, as no one can actually understand his accent!

Big, strong neck

Slight beard

Sporran

Surprisingly small feet

Hair tied in bunches

Full beard

MacGuffin clan tartan

Strong arms

Lord MacGuffin

King Fergus once saved MacGuffin from a deadly arrow. MacGuffin repaid the favour by helping Fergus in his first battle with Mor'du. Now, MacGuffin has his heart set on his son marrying Fergus's daughter.

BRAVE

CLAN DINGWALL's men are not renowned for their height or brawn. However, what they lack in stature, they make up for in spirit. Lord Dingwall and his son have the same hair, but Wee Dingwall's temper is not fiery like his father's.

Proud dad
As Lord Dingwall boasts about his son, the rest of the clans look impressed, until the real Wee Dingwall steps out from behind the muscly warrior.

Wild hair

Wee Dingwall
Wee Dingwall isn't tall, or strong or clever, but he has other skills. When given a bow, he would rather pluck it like a harp than shoot an arrow.

Oversized sporran

Skinny legs

Dingwall clan tartan

Lord Dingwall
Lord Dingwall is proud of his son and likes to boast about all of his achievements. Although Wee Dingwall doesn't quite live up to expectations, his dad still wants him to marry Princess Merida.

YOUNG MACINTOSH AND LORD MACINTOSH

CLAN MACINTOSH come from the remote Isle of Skye. The wiry warriors like to look tough, so they don't even wear undershirts! Lord Macintosh and his son might want to look fierce, but underneath the war paint, they are just big crybabies.

Skinny body

Blue war paint

Proud expression

Macintosh family tartan

Large sword

Mace

Young Macintosh

Young Macintosh loves to show off and is used to being cheered by crowds of adoring ladies. However, when Merida chooses an archery contest to decide her suitor, the would-be warrior soon shows his true colours.

Boastful dad
Lord Macintosh loves to tell tall tales about his son's achievements, including the time he vanquished 1,000 foes with his sword!

Lord Macintosh

Lord Macintosh likes to look the part of the tough warrior, but, as with his son, his appearance is deceptive. The lanky Lord is extremely suspicious and always thinks that he is being treated unfairly.

"Och, we've all heard that tale!"

Lord Macintosh

RILEY

RILEY ANDERSEN is a regular, happy, 11-year-old girl who loves her family, her friends and ice hockey. Not too much riles Riley. She's positive and smart, and spends most of her time smiling. But when life starts to get complicated, her personality starts to change!

Going for the goal
Just like her dad, Riley is totally hooked on ice hockey. She loves playing for her team, the Prairie Dogs. Riley has been scoring goals on the ice since she was a little girl.

Home in Minnesota
Riley has grown up in a comfortable house in Minnesota. She loves her home and has never lived anywhere else...

Best friends
Riley's lifelong best friend is Meg. They've been laughing together ever since they were little. Once Meg made Riley laugh so hard that milk actually came out of her nose!

Did You Know?
In Minnesota, Riley goes ice skating on her local lake whenever it freezes over.

Amazing imagination
From a bright pink imaginary friend named Bing Bong to a volcano spitting lava in her living room, Riley has always had a very vivid imagination. Her highly active mind means that even the most mundane day can be transformed into an exciting adventure!

Scuffed trainers

JOY

AS THE MOST OPTIMISTIC of the Emotions, Joy is always happy and hopeful. With her sunny outlook, she is able to see the positive in everything. Joy never gives up on her aim to make Riley happy every single day. So far, she has been pretty successful!

Joy enjoys
Joy loves special golden memories, goofing around and group hugs. But more than anything, she adores Riley's smile.

Glowing, golden memory sphere

Head Emotion
As their unofficial leader, Joy keeps the other Emotions organised and on track. While they are very glad Joy's in charge, she can be a little bossy sometimes!

"I've got a great idea!"

Pride and Joy
All the Emotions want Riley to be happy, so Joy is usually the one at the controls. But she doesn't realise that it's natural for Riley to sometimes feel sad.

Positive plans
Joy works very hard to try and keep Riley cheerful. She watches carefully for warning signs of potential downers around the corner. Just in case things go wrong, she always has a back-up plan!

Cheerful, flowery dress

SADNESS

SADNESS OFTEN FINDS herself feeling thoroughly miserable. This pessimistic Emotion can never look on the bright side. But being sad isn't all bad. Sadness helps Riley feel better about moving to San Francisco by letting her have a good cry.

Tearful, not cheerful

Joy is always trying to get Sadness to be more optimistic – without success! When her efforts fail, Joy puts the miserable Emotion in a Circle of Sadness and tells her to stay inside. That way, she can't spread her gloominess.

"It's like I'm having a breakdown!"

Did You Know?

In her spare time, Sadness reads many of the mind manuals in Headquarters.

Sombre expression

Weepy world

Sadness doesn't want to feel down all the time, but she just can't seem to help it. There is so much to weep about in the world, from losing toys to watching sandcastles collapse!

Negative touch

Sadness has a habit of turning the brightest moments into gloomy situations. Each time she touches one of Riley's happy memories, it turns sad and blue.

Sadness is always blue – in colour and in mood

FEAR

FEAR IS FRIGHTENED of almost everything, but he is proud that by being constantly scared, he has saved Riley from the perils of the world. Fear does feel shaky most of the time, but you won't shake him from his belief that ultra-cautious is the only way to be.

Did You Know?
Fear prepares a long list of potential disasters before any big event in Riley's life.

"I'm so jumpy! My nerves are shot."

Eyes wide open in shock

Quitter
When the going gets tough inside Headquarters, Fear tries to run away.

Nervous wreck
After arriving in San Francisco and hearing about the area's earthquakes, Fear is even more jumpy than usual. Now even the slightest surprise reduces him to a trembling mess.

100% nonscary knitwear

Fear in charge
Fear is always on the lookout for potential hazards, such as low-hanging power cords. Over the years, he has saved Riley from some pretty nasty accidents.

Scare care
None of the other Emotions understand how dangerous the world can be! Fear believes that being scared is not necessarily a bad thing. Whenever Riley feels scared, she pays attention to her surroundings and is extra careful, which keeps her safe.

Legs often used for running away

ANGER

ANGER HAS some serious issues with his bad temper. He gets furious every time he thinks things are not fair for Riley. This overreacting Emotion believes in justice, but he also believes in screaming, shouting and throwing chairs!

All the rage

When Anger is at the console, Riley becomes pretty irritable. You can expect rude remarks, a lot of rash decisions and plenty of drama!

Anger's idea

Anger is not usually a smiley kind of a guy. However, when he picks out an idea bulb, for once he is pleased rather than peeved. He is sure that this will help fix all of Riley's problems.

Hot head

When Anger reaches his boiling point, bright flames shoot out of his head! The other Emotions have sometimes had to use an extinguisher to put out his fires!

"Now for a few well-placed withering scowls!"

Think second

Anger is impatient and impulsive. His reaction to feeling frustrated is to fight first and think second. While problems may be quickly resolved, it also leads to trouble and tantrums!

Teeth gritted in frustration

Fingers curled in rage

Did You Know?

Anger is dying to try out any new swear words he learns as Riley grows up.

DISGUST

DISGUST BELIEVES the world is riddled with foul odors, toxic tastes and poisonous people. With so much dirt, disease and bad fashion in the world, Disgust keeps Riley safe by warning her of every possible poison.

Difficult attitude
With her strong opinions and attitude, Disgust can come across as abrupt and aloof. Thankfully, the other Emotions are used to her sarcastic tone!

"I'm gonna be sick..."

Always right
Disgust sticks to strict beliefs about what food should look like or which clothes are uncool. That's because she views her own great taste as a gift – one that has saved Riley from being grossed-out on many occasions.

Did You Know?
Disgust thinks that cities are horrible, dirty places – they should always be avoided!

Stylish neckerchief

Unimpressed body language

In control
When danger looms, Disgust is always ready to grab the controls. Her quick thinking has saved Riley from many disgusting incidents!

Sassy stance

For Riley
Like all of the Emotions, Disgust always has Riley's best interests at heart. As she watches the view screen in Headquarters, it is obvious just how much she cares.

MUM AND DAD

IN MANY WAYS, Jill and Bill Andersen are the perfect parents. They are proud of their daughter and have given their only child a happy and loving childhood. But Riley is growing up fast. She won't be their happy-go-lucky little girl forever. Life is definitely about to get a lot more interesting for this family!

Family fun
The Andersens love goofing around and making each other laugh. They can't imagine any problem they couldn't overcome with a bit of fun family time.

Sand man
Riley's dad is a really good sport. He even allowed Riley to bury him in the sand at the beach. It's lucky she stopped at his neck!

Did You Know?
Mum's Emotions all wear red glasses and Dad's Emotions all have moustaches.

Fashionable red glasses

Big, goofy smile

Sensible business clothes

Mum and Dad's dream
Riley's parents both have a sense of adventure. Dad has always dreamed of starting his own company in San Francisco and Mum shares his excitement about a new start in a new city.

Hockey mum
Riley's mum is her daughter's biggest supporter. At every ice hockey game, she's there rooting for Riley and cheering her on from the bleachers.

BING BONG

FUN-LOVING BING BONG was once Riley's imaginary friend. They used to play together all the time. But ever since Riley turned four, her cuddly companion has been without a job and playmate. Now he's determined to get back to being Riley's best friend again!

Did You Know?
This sweet-natured creature cries tears of candy and leaves a trail of them wherever he goes.

"I'm all set to take Riley to the moon!"

Elephant's trunk

Way back
When Bing Bong bumps into Joy and Sadness in Long Term Memory, he vows to help them find their way back to Headquarters. He hopes Joy can help Riley remember him, too.

Dream drama
In a desperate bid to be remembered by Riley, Bing Bong boldly sneaks into a scene in one of her dreams. He just wants to get noticed!

Body made out of candy floss

Cat's tail

Imaginary mayhem
Riley and Bing Bong enjoyed hours of crazy games. These included time travel and races on the ceiling! But best of all were the trips in Bing Bong's song-powered wagon rocket.

ARLO

ARLO IS NOT your average Apatosaurus. The young dino is nervous about the big world around him. Despite being jumpy and jittery, Arlo does his best to fit in. He is friendly, fun-loving and always willing to help his folks on the farm!

Did You Know?

Arlo is the youngest dino in the family by just a few seconds. He was the last egg to hatch, after his sister Libby and his brother Buck.

Clumsy claws

Arlo can be pretty clumsy – the gangly and awkward Apatosaurus is forever taking a tumble! It seems that Arlo can't do anything on the farm without tripping over or spilling something!

A strong will

Arlo might be a little timid, but he has more than a little spirit. The young dino is determined to help out on the farm, even if it means feeding the terrifying chickens.

Shell-shocked

When Arlo hatches, his parents are surprised to find such a tiny dino inside a huge egg! However, his size doesn't matter – they love him just the way he is.

"I ain't a coward! And I'm gonna make my mark!"

Wobbly legs prone to stumbling

Feet often used for running away from things

POPPA AND MOMMA

POPPA AND MOMMA work as a team – looking after their family, their farm, and each other. The devoted dinos lead a peaceful and happy life, but it can be hard. Every harvest must be a success for the family to survive!

Poppa is the tallest in the family

A strong bond
Arlo may get scared easily, but he knows that Poppa will always protect him. Poppa does everything he can to help his son get over his fears and feel safe on the farm.

Poppa
Poppa shows great strength, both in his powerful body and in his determination to take care of his family. The resilient reptile remains focused and fearless, never giving up on anything or anyone!

Ultra-long neck for plowing

Momma
Warm-hearted Momma keeps the family going. Her love and good humour make every day feel better. However, it is her grit and spirit that allow the family to live at the farm year after year.

Momma is skilled at seeding the fields

Did You Know?
Poppa and Momma's first names are actually Henry and Ida.

Passing on wisdom
Poppa and Momma keep a watchful eye on their children. The proud and patient parents teach their little ones everything they know about the world.

LIBBY AND BUCK

ARLO'S BIG BROTHER and sister, Buck and Libby, work hard on the farm. They are eager to make Momma and Poppa proud. They also love joking around – especially when it involves teasing Arlo!

Libby

Libby is always playing tricks – she loves hiding and then surprising her brothers. The looks on their faces never fail to make the playful prankster laugh.

Playful prankster

Buck takes his chores very seriously, but he also finds time to mess around. But when he tricks Arlo, things can get a little heated.

"You mess up your chores, and everyone else's!"

Buck

Buck can be hot-headed sometimes. When Arlo messes up his chores, his big brother calls him a coward! Arlo is determined to prove him wrong.

Hard workers

Chores are a very important part of farm life. Libby and Buck excel at them, quickly earning the right to "make their mark".

Long, graceful neck

Dark green stripes across Libby's back

Powerful tail for knocking down trees

Strong legs help Buck carry logs

SPOT

HUMAN BOY SPOT is clever, courageous and an expert at surviving in the wild! Separated from his family early on, Spot has taught himself how to hunt, hide and build a shelter. He has also learned to never give up!

Super sniffer
Spot's time in the wild has given him an amazing sense of smell. His super-sensitive nose can follow a scent for miles. This is a gift that is not to be sniffed at!

"Howwwwwwllllllllll!"

Leaves in hair for camouflage

Did You Know?
Spot moves around on all fours and can't speak the way that Arlo can! Spot uses grunts, growls and howls to communicate with others.

Strong arms and legs for running and climbing

A spot of company
Although Spot has grown up on his own, the young loner actually enjoys hanging out with other creatures. In fact, once you gain his trust, Spot is a fiercely loyal and lovable friend.

Firefly fun
Curious Spot is never afraid of meeting new creatures. He is fascinated by the glowing fireflies and skillfully manages to capture one so that he can take a closer look.

THUNDERCLAP

TERRIFYING PTERODACTYL

Thunderclap leads a gang of winged scavengers. These fearless fliers believe that storms can provide anything – including food. They glide through the skies and swoop down to gobble up wounded critters, stopping at nothing to catch their prey.

Thunderclap's gang

Downpour, Coldfront, Frostbite and Windgust are all named after the storm. They may belong to one gang, but when it comes to food, they fight each other for every last scrap!

Storm follower

Weather-obsessed Thunderclap believes that the storm has special powers. He thinks that it gave him a "relevation", which made him fearless.

— Wide wingspan for gliding

Large head crest

Did You Know?

Thunderclap made up the word "relevation" to talk about how the storm took him from a low point in his life to a high point.

Sharp talons for snatching helpless critters

Meet and eat

When Arlo first meets Thunderclap after a storm, the Pterodactyl seems friendly and helpful. However, the ruthless predator is only interested in eating Spot!

"The storm gave me a relevation and I wasn't scared anymore."

NASH AND RAMSEY

FROM AN EARLY AGE, siblings Nash and Ramsey help their father, Butch, with herding longhorns. Growing up together has made them good friends, but there is still more than a little sibling rivalry!

Scare pair
Nash and Ramsey work together to leave their foes frozen with terror! They waste no time fighting off the Pterodactyls that attack Spot and Arlo.

Big softies
At first, Arlo is terrified of these fearsome T. rexes, but he quickly realises that they're more friendly than ferocious!

> "Nash! Boundaries!
> This is my personal bubble."
>
> Ramsey

Ramsey
Smart and quick-witted, Ramsey is as sharp as one of her claws! Very little rattles Ramsey – she loves the challenge of keeping longhorns in line.

Ultra-tough skin

Nash is usually smiling

Nash
Laid-back Nash isn't the brightest dinosaur out on the range. He spends most of his time daydreaming, when he should be keeping an eye on the longhorns!

Razor-sharp claws

BUTCH

T. REXES ARE the fiercest dinosaurs around – and Nash and Ramsey's father, Butch, is no exception! The tough-talking rancher might not be very touchy-feely, but Butch does have a softer side.

Old battle scar on jaw

Doting dad

Butch is proud of Nash and Ramsey. They help him herd the longhorns. By learning on the job, they can follow in his (enormous) footsteps!

Veteran rancher

Butch is one of the best ranchers in the region. His years of experience, combined with his flair for scaring rustlers, make him the last T. rex you should mess with!

"If you're pullin' my leg, I'm gonna eat yours!"

Gruesome grin

Butch is a dino of few words, and Arlo finds it hard to tell what he's thinking. Is that a gruesome grin or a frightening frown? With those teeth, it's just best to stay out of his way!

Huge feet with sharp claws

Did You Know?

Butch still has a croc tooth lodged in his jaw from a croc attack that happened many years ago!

RAPTOR PACK

RAPTORS ARE the most despised dinosaurs around! These dim-witted fiends spend their time rustling longhorns and threatening prey. Raptors are small, but when they attack, they are speedy, savage and seriously dangerous!

Did You Know?
The raptors are ferocious, and will fight anyone who gets in their way.

Earl
Earl is a very dim dino, who is very quick to anger.

Earl is covered in dirty feathers

Bubbha
Bubbha is the unofficial leader of the pack of raptors. The other three will do what he says!

Tail of dirty, blue feathers

Very big teeth

Pervis
Pervis is desperate to impress Bubbha, but he's not interested.

Nasty look on her face

Gang of thieves
Bubbha, Pervis, Earl and Lurleane are a really unpleasant pack. The fearsome four think nothing of stealing the T. rexes' herd of longhorns for themselves.

Lurleane
Lurleane is the only female in Bubbha's gang. She's intent on catching and hurting Arlo.

217

MIGUEL

THIS TALENTED 12-year-old's greatest passion is music. The trouble is, his family hates music, and it is banned from the Rivera household. Miguel doesn't want to fight with his family, but can he find a way to bring music back to his home?

Family photo
In an old family photo, Miguel finds his great-great grandfather holding a guitar just like Ernesto de la Cruz's. Were his family once musicians? Miguel shouts excitedly from the rooftops!

"I gotta seize my moment!"

Carved skull on guitar's headstock

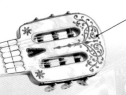

Music crazy
A magical mishap takes Miguel to another land. There, he gets the chance to prove he can be a musician… and to meet his idol, Ernesto de la Cruz!

Boots made by the Rivera family

Talent contest
Miguel's heart leaps when he sees the poster for a Día de los Muertos talent show in the village plaza. Could this be his chance to follow his musical destiny?

DANTE

THIS GOOFY street dog loves to follow Miguel around. He's a hairless Mexican Xoloitzcuintli – but you can call him a Xolo for short! Curious, friendly and unable to resist a new smell, Dante seems to pop up whenever Miguel is about to have an adventure.

Street survivor
This scrappy hound has learned to survive on the street. He'll sniff any bag for food and even dance for a sweet bread roll!

"Never name a street dog. They'll follow you forever."
Abuelita

Sharing secrets
Dante is the only friend Miguel can tell all his hopes and dreams to – and sing all his favourite songs with. Shh!

Loco Xolo?
He may look like a crazy critter, but Dante has hidden depths. After all, he is a Xolo dog, and it is said that all Xolo dogs have secret, mysterious powers.

Dying for a snack
Ever-hungry Dante can't stop chasing food, even in the Land of the Dead. Well, the catering there is classier than in the alleys back home...

Strong, smooth, hairless skin

Paws toughened by padding the streets

COCO

FINDING OUT that his family is even bigger than he thought is a shock for Miguel. Discovering that his ancestors hate music just as much as the others is even more of a shock. There must be somebody who can help Miguel make sense of it all (not to mention make his way home). Will it be his old folks, his new friends or his big musical hero?

Comfy slippers

Coco

Miguel's great grandmother, Coco, was once full of interesting stories. Now that she is very old, she has forgotten most of them.

Papá   **Mamá**   **Abuelita**

Family trade

Miguel comes from a big family, and all of them are skilled shoemakers. The trade is passed on from generation to generation.

Did You Know?

De la Cruz was a movie star, as well as a musician. He specialised in heroic and romantic roles.

Showy, large-brimmed hat

Ornate patterns decorate his guitar

Ernesto de la Cruz

De la Cruz is still a hero to the people of Santa Cecilia. His melodic crooning really put their little town on the map.

Neatly styled hair

Embroidered pinafore

No-nonsense stance

Abuelita

Miguel's grandmother, Abuelita, is kind and sweet... until Miguel mentions music. Then, she turns into a fierce and forbidding adversary.

Mamá Imelda

Mamá Imelda is Miguel's great-great grandmother. She started the family shoemaking business to support herself and her daughter, Coco.

Flounced skirt

Stretched-out suspenders

Héctor

Héctor is worried that he will soon be forgotten forever. He makes a bargain with Miguel to keep his memory alive.

Ragged pants

Identical hat to brother's

Shoemaker's leather apron

Riveras Family

The skeleton Riveras haven't changed much from when they were alive. Brothers Óscar and Felipe still wear their leather aprons, and they still do what their big sister Imelda says.

Tío Óscar   **Tío Felipe**

INDEX

Page numbers in **bold** indicate main entries.

Editors Ellie Barton, Jo Casey, Beth Davies, Helen Murray
Designers Richard Horsford, Poppy Joslin, David McDonald,
Satvir Sihota, Lisa Sodeau, Rhys Thomas
Pre-Producer Siu Chan
Producer Louise Daly
Managing Editor Paula Regan
Managing Art Editor Jo Connor
Art Director Lisa Lanzarini
Publisher Julie Ferris
Publishing Director Simon Beecroft

Written by Steve Bynghall, Jo Casey, Glenn Dakin, Clare Hibbert,
Julia March, Helen Murray and Catherine Saunders

This edition published in 2019
First published in Great Britain in 2012 by
Dorling Kindersley Limited
80 Strand, London WC2R 0RL
A Penguin Random House Company

10 9 8 7 6 5 4 3 2 1
001–315169–May/2019

Page design copyright © 2019 Dorling Kindersley Limited

A CIP catalogue record for this book is available from the British Library.

ISBN 978-0-24139-245-4

Acknowledgements
The publisher would like to thank Kayla Dugger, Pamela Afram, Emma Grange, Julia March
and Victoria Taylor at DK for editorial assistance; Lynne Moulding at DK for design assistance;
and Chelsea Alon, Chuck Wilson, Scott Tilley and Tony Fejeran at Disney Publishing.

Printed and bound in China

www.dk.com
www.disney.com

A WORLD OF IDEAS:
SEE ALL THERE IS TO KNOW